D1503216

Advance Praise for *Jesus & Co.*

"Really interesting book and very well written. Bruce uses the historical Jesus to play out the many facets of business in a unique way to tell the story. This coupled with the blending of a personally powerful story makes for a unique and interesting story."

–STEVE STRAUSS, author and syndicated columnist

"Welcome to the Marketplace and the Messiah. Here, in the company of Jesus, Networker, Delegator, Team Builder, and Borrower, you'll discover the best practices of the gospel as lived out in the aisles and corporate headquarters of America. In *Jesus & Co.*, Hartman, famed CFO of Foot Locker, shares his own search for a productive career as he walks his readers toward the One who is the Way, the truth, and the life. Blessings on the Way."

–DR. HEATHER MURRAY ELKINS, author of *Holy Stuff of Life*

"As a Christ follower and business owner, I can tell you that every single word in this book has immense value. You can learn a ton from Bruce's workplace experience, personal faith, and God-given insight. A must-read!"

–BRYAN MILES, Founder and CEO of Belay

What Bruce Hartman has done in *Jesus & Co.*—and it's no small accomplishment—is take the stories of Jesus and retell them in a way that not only makes them particularly relevant to the modern business world, but also reinforces their meaning for everyone."

–RICHARD WILLETT, award-winning playwright and editor of *Proof of Heaven*

"Bruce Hartman presents a persuasive argument in a well written format. I would expect nothing less. In the book *Jesus & Co.*, Bruce invites the reader into his life as a senior officer in several Fortune 500 companies, while wrestling with the relevance of his faith as a Christian to his professional life. Drawing on his considerable body of work and, at the same time, drawing on the spiritual resources and challenges of the Gospel of Jesus Christ, he gives insight to what it means to be a person of faith in every corner of one's life. Bruce has given us another Jesus. He has made Jesus relevant to our lives. This book is evangelism at its finest."

–DR. VIRGINIA SAMUEL, Former Associate Dean
of Drew University Theological School

"Bravo! Great book full of wonderful life lessons about Jesus, the Apostles, and the contemporary workplace. Bruce provides an excellent view of the connection of today's marketplace with Jesus's marketplace. A great guide for anyone searching to 'balance' themselves, especially in today's business world. A must-read for any business executive looking to be successful ethically and professionally!"

–MIKE ZAWOSKY, Former CEO of Shoe Sensation

"Congratulations to Bruce Hartman for writing a unique book that explains how many of the challenges that he encountered during his distinguished career in the business world were successfully resolved using tactics that were in line with the key messages from the teachings of Jesus Christ. Having worked for Bruce during most of his years at Foot Locker, I can attest to his distinct management style that empowered others to 'take charge,' his insistence that everyone 'focus on what counts' and to do so in a way that was ethically sound. His leadership style and the management process he employed were instrumental in getting the organization to capitalize on many opportunities that led to Foot Locker's ongoing success. In fact, many of the management processes that were developed during his years at Foot Locker are still used by the company today."

–PETER BROWN, Former CIO and Treasurer of Foot Locker

"Bruce is an amazing life mentor. I have been lucky enough to learn from him for five years now in every discipline from private life to my career. He has a distinct way of balancing building one's enthusiasm with teaching the importance of authenticity and morality. He is a holistic visionary and master detail examiner, an expert at every level of business from processing raw numbers to understanding the social impacts of business decisions. I am honored to have Bruce as a close friend and teacher. Anyone would be lucky to have a chance to learn from Bruce."

–DAN CASTELLANO, UX Evangelist

"Bruce is among the most insightful and innovative executives I have worked under. He was a key leader of the turnaround at Foot Locker. He drives innovation, challenges the team to think harder to generate ideas, and provides the leadership to execute the plan. He has played a significant role in the development of many executives' careers over the years, including mine."

–RYAN MALLORY, VP Ross Stores

"A mentor is someone who has achieved the success that you want...someone who can help lead the way, encourage, and push you beyond what you thought you were capable of doing. For me, that was Bruce Hartman and I thank him for the wonderful journey, and congrats on a wonderful book."

–BEN MENEZES, CFO Popcornopolis

"Bruce is one of the brightest financial executives I have worked with. He was excellent at driving productivity improvement programs and cash optimization strategies. He is also an experienced change agent, who helped drive a positive transformation of Yankee Candle."

–HARLAN KENT, CEO Performance Sports Group

"Bruce has a broad and deep knowledge of business in general and, more specifically, of the companies he worked for, and fully understands the interdependence across functions He has been a driving force in several turn-arounds or corporate transformations. His single-minded focus and his will to execute made him an effective and successful executive."

–JIM SUTLIFFE, VP HRSC retail

"Bruce is a unique individual with a creative and innovative approach to getting things accomplished. Surgical in his approach to ascertaining the issues surrounding opportunities and any roadblocks standing in the way of progress. Possessing a tireless dedication to building an organization with sound and moral fundamentals, while ensuring the proper talent is brought to the process."

–FRAN CLERKIN, CEO BSP

"Extremely effective leader who excels at organizational development and motivating his team. Bruce is the best change agent I've have experienced. He was the primary reason Foot Locker was able to avoid bankruptcy."

–PETER CUPPS, Former VP Foot Locker

"The mark of any great leader is the scorecard of people that he nurtured, promoted, and helped along the way. I can think of no less than a dozen executives that Bruce directly managed and mentored who have gone on to significant executive positions in other companies."

–MIKE POWELL, CEO Mark Allen

"Bruce is one of the most dynamic and passionate executives I've encountered in my career. His passion to drive change and rally the team is contagious. He is intelligent and has a broad knowledge base which provides him the capacity to rapidly discern the pertinent points and make quick decisions."

–REGGIE THOMAS, VP Yankee Candle

"I was hired by Bruce one year out of college. Through Bruce's management—and constant guidance—I learned the importance of planning and how to be a focused. He taught me what it meant to really work hard...and he always worked harder than those who worked with him. I learned from Bruce how to give people a chance to rise to the occasion and shine. Through it all, Bruce remained upbeat and patient. He gave me a great foundation that has served me well through the years ... I am fortunate to have worked with Bruce."

–BARBARA CHAMBERS, Senior Engagement Officer, Alzheimer's Fund

"The relationship between Christianity and capitalism is fraught and complicated. Yet, in this thought-provoking book Bruce Hartman gives us a hopeful way of following Jesus in the marketplace with integrity and faithfulness. Christian leadership requires a rootedness that is also principally adaptable. Hartman show us how to do so with probity and character."

–JAVIER A. VIERA, Vice Provost, Dean of the Theological School, and Professor of Pastoral Theology and Leadership, Drew University

"Bruce Hartman explores how and why the god of the market is a false god, but Jesus in the marketplace is true and to be trusted. Be moved, challenged, instructed, and inspired by this supremely satisfying and brimful book."

–LEONARD SWEET, bestselling author, speaker, and founder of preachthestory.com

JESUS & CO.

JESUS & CO.

Connecting the Lessons of The Gospel with Today's Business World

BRUCE L. HARTMAN

A POST HILL PRESS BOOK

Jesus & Co.:
Connecting the Lessons of The Gospel with Today's Business World
© 2018 by Bruce L. Hartman
All Rights Reserved

ISBN: 978-1-68261-547-8
ISBN (eBook): 978-1-68261-548-5

Cover art by Payton Grant
Interior design and composition by Greg Johnson, Textbook Perfect

All Bible verses were selected from the New Revised Standard Version (NRSV).

Post Hill Press
New York • Nashville
posthillpress.com

Published in the United States of America

TABLE OF CONTENTS

PREFACE

"Father, if you are willing, take this cup from me; yet not my will, but yours be done."

–LUKE 22:42

Late at night in an ancient Judean garden, a man in his early thirties asked, ***"Are you sure this is the only way?"***[1]

It was the third time that evening the young man had returned to the garden, each time with the same request: ***"Are you sure?"***

He was met by silence, but the answer was clear. The fullness of his humanity exposed, he was sweating to the point of bleeding. ***"Not my will but yours,"*** he reluctantly assented. He knew what lay ahead. Betrayal by his friends and humiliation in front of his community. An agonizing beating that would tear the skin from his back. A trek carrying his cross to a hill. Death by crucifixion. All this he and he alone had to undergo in order to connect humanity with God. In fact, he was creating a flower for humankind called Easter.

Many times in our work life, we face difficult choices, such as the choice between acquiescence to an unethical request from a boss

---

[1] *Note:* Words actually spoken by Jesus are italicized in bold within the chapters.

or colleague and doing what's right. We are frequently tempted to take the easy way, to relieve the pressure on ourselves, to dispel the tension, to avoid the moment of having to deliver a tough message to our superiors and to disobey them. The walk to the boss's office will seem endless. Each breath and thought will hang thickly around us, almost choking us. But we have a choice; we can do the ethical thing, and we have the example above, of Jesus in the Garden of Gethsemane on that fateful night, to show why this is the choice we should make.

Consider Sherron Watkins, who delivered the bad news about Enron to her employers. Her act was costly. She became a pariah within the company; scorned by Enron's management, she lived a difficult, lonely life. There may have come a time when she wondered whether it had been worth her bravery. Her internal moral compass, not a desire for fame, had driven her to tell the truth and seek a way to repair the damage. And as time passed, and the issues she revealed came fully to light, she became a model for corporate integrity. In 2001, she was named one of *Time* magazine's People of the Year.

Confronting such challenges is an everyday job. In our workplace, tough and uneasy decisions have to be made. But we are fortunate to have the example of Jesus in the garden to serve as our model. Through daily prayers and our relationship with God, we can become emboldened and confident in our decision making. No longer should we fear the pain often associated with a tough decision; we can carry on, sure in our faith that God is with us.

Many of us know Jesus from Sunday school, or the way he's portrayed in the media, or from what our friends have told us. Most of these projections portray the human form of Jesus as a great rabbi, a sage of spirituality. But if we look closely at history and the Bible, we will find a richer and more complicated Jesus. He was, after all, a skilled carpenter. He knew and became an authentic member of the world most of us work in.

Most of his human contacts were from the marketplace. Of his nearly fifty parables, the vast majority relate to Judean farmers, shepherds, craftsmen, artisans, tax collectors, and street merchants. In the four Gospels, Jesus appeared in public 132 times; over 120 of those appearances were in the marketplace. Jesus had enough contacts where he worked that he could borrow a donkey from a local merchant and a room for his only committee meeting, the Last Supper.

Many sources, including our English Bible, refer to Jesus as a carpenter. Granted, it is hard to imagine Jesus as a worker, but he did submit himself to being fully human. When we look at the earliest Greek versions of the Bible, the word *tekton* appears, meaning "artisan." All sources show he was a skilled member of the first-century marketplace.

After working in this capacity in Judea, he began a three-year mission to join humankind with God. He moved about Judea and Galilee, preaching to marketplace people. Jesus knew the struggles of the workers, not only in daily life, but also with the ethical issues many confronted. Most of the same issues we deal with today existed in this ancient marketplace.

Today's marketplace needs Jesus. His absence—or our lack of attention to and understanding of his teachings—has made most of us think of investment banks, hedge funds, insurance companies, car manufacturers, and businesses of every kind as corrupt, amoral, without compassion, and in some cases we are right.

Volkswagen declares it has lowered its emission rate by forty times and creates a worldwide uproar when the claim is shown to be not true. The result: a fifteen-billion-dollar payment to compensate for the company's lie. The *Exxon Valdez* spills millions of gallons of oil onto the Pacific coast and Exxon fights for years to avoid paying penalties. A British Petroleum oil rig explodes in the Gulf of Mexico, endangering wildlife, fisheries, the entire economy of the region, and its management denies culpability, blaming others, desperately seeking to hold down its financial cost. Michael Milken uses stock manipulation to enrich himself, though it costs his clients millions. Bernard Madoff runs a Ponzi scheme for decades, until he is caught, often costing whoever invested with him their savings. Occidental Chemical dumps their poisonous waste into rivers and streams in upstate New York and, thanks to clever and expensive lawyers, wins the suit brought against them.

I think it unlikely that Jesus would approve.

These scandals make headlines, and we react with outrage, shock, dismay, horror, and, yes, a sense of self-satisfaction: How awful, how immoral, that powerful people and powerful companies can literally get away with murder. *We* would never let such things to happen. *We* are good, God-fearing people, incapable of such dishonesty.

Are we? Workers in the marketplace like you and (formerly) me are every day faced with moral decisions on a smaller scale, the answers to which will or will not align themselves with the teachings of Jesus.

Fudge the figures, a CEO demands; hide the flaws in our product, see what you can find out about our rival's finances, even if you have to bribe someone to do it. Spy on your coworker; lie to your sales force or customers; assure the public that there's nothing wrong even when there is.

In the abstract such moral choices (I *won't* massage the figures...I *won't* spy on Ralph) are easy. But in practice, when doing the moral thing is what Jesus would wish but might cost you your job, the choice is more difficult. Whistle-blowers are forever in jeopardy of losing their jobs, and any confrontation with your bosses, even when you know they are wrong, is hazardous. The question of whether to obey or resist faces us at all the levels of the company.

When we go along, when the whistle stays silent in our mouths, when we are complicit in subterfuge, we are compromised, humiliated, untrue to ourselves and to Jesus. A sense of incompleteness follows—frustration, a reduction in self-esteem, and the diminishment of self-worth. Our hearts are roiled.

At times we become tempted through our own desires. We need to hit a number we promised our bosses, so we bend the rules. We need to make the sale, so we conceal important facts from our customers. We feel that if we reach a little farther than we should, it will be okay, just this one time. We give in to temptation to alleviate fear or gain an advantage.

In the garden where Jesus was praying, he went back three times to the three apostles he had brought with him, and found them asleep. *"The spirit is willing but the flesh is weak,"* he famously said, summing up the human condition: that we are all good at heart, but are prone to the temptations of the world. When we finally enter the world of the spirit and listen to the model of Jesus, our hearts are eased.

We might turn to the church, but our churches have become less relevant—every major study shows a decline in attendance over the past few decades. Of the 120 million Americans in the marketplace who identify themselves as Christians, over ninety million don't go to church and are thus left morally and spiritually unattended. The church has not changed to address the needs of those in the workforce of the contemporary marketplace and is often caught up in meaningless fights over dogma, personal ambition, or politics. The religious elite, far too often fighting for power than for God, has become similar to that of the ancient Judean society. This form of religiosity only serves to scare people away from Christ.

Driven by salacious stories about CEOs and CFOs, the media paints a bleak picture of the marketplace to generate ad revenues, not to tell the whole truth. This portrayal misses that the vast majority of workers, who want to perform ethically, are viewed as a collection of "soulless creatures" by the church. They are left to rely on charlatans, loud voices from the fringe seeking fame, to receive their lessons in faith.

Local clergy are burdened as well, hemmed in by the religious elite who impose excessive bureaucratic and doctrinal boundaries. Our local pastors face an insurmountable task in defending faith against an onslaught of misinformation. They face excessively loud parishioners, who hang on to the past and won't allow the local pastor to change the local church to meet the demands of a contemporary marketplace in which, for example, both parents often work. And, like the worker in the marketplace, they work endless hours that put pressure on their health and families. They are underpaid for tending to their flock. True, there are some who don't live up to their calling, but they don't represent the majority who labor in silence. Their calling and the church itself are vital to the marketplace and need to be raised up. The Pharisees of today need to be held off.

This book isn't about "believe or be doomed." It is about a journey with Jesus. A walk with Jesus that reveals God's values for our personal and work lives. It is for the vast unserved community of the marketplace looking for a way to create straight moral paths in their work and personal lives. It is for those seeking a change in their hearts to pursue God's way and God himself. For we follow God with our hearts and souls. It is our egos that pursue the world's temptations.

I've structured the book by interweaving stories of faithful people, events from my own life, and most importantly the words and life of

Jesus. The book is designed to show others how to handle the inevitable ethical struggles of the workplace. And to show how central Jesus's message was for the contemporary worker in the marketplace of his time—and ours.

Is it possible to follow Jesus's teachings and remain a loyal, productive, respected, and self-respecting worker? Can we thrive and stay true to the words of Christ? My answer is a resounding YES and my purpose in this book is to show you how.

CHAPTER 1

JESUS AND MARKETPLACE VALUES

"'You shall love the Lord your God with all your heart, and with all your soul, and with all your mind.' This is the greatest and first command-ment. And a second is like it: 'You shall love your neighbor as yourself.' On these two commandments hang all the law and the prophets."

−MATTHEW 22:37−40

Jesus was a man of the marketplace and not the overly romanticized figure of contemporary thought. Commerce was different in his time; fishing was a well-respected profession, farming was a necessity for most families, and shepherds dotted the hillsides. There were no banks, no stock markets, only rudimentary "hedge funds." Most com-merce was carried out near or in temples, such as the Court of the Gentiles, part of the majestic temple in ancient Jerusalem. The mar-ketplace was as important in Judean times as it is now, and it seems that the moral issues were similar to ours.

Jesus frequently appeared in the marketplace, and his parables are about the marketplace in everyday life; the parable of the talents

(Matthew 25:14–30) and the parable of the evil farmers (Luke 20:9–19) are prime examples. In these parables and sermons, Jesus stressed a morality based on serving God or doing God's will, and treating our neighbor, fairly.

"What is the most important of all the Commandments?" asked the religious elite. *Jesus*, who almost never answered such a question with a straight answer (he used parables, letting his listeners arrive at the answers themselves), this time answered directly. *"'You should love the Lord your God with all your heart, and with all your soul, and with all your mind.' This is the greatest and first commandment. And a second is like it: 'You shall love your neighbor as yourself.' On these two commandments hang all the law and the prophets."* (Matthew 22:37–40)

In the parable of the Good Samaritan (Luke 10:25–37), Jesus illustrates what makes a good neighbor. He describes a Samaritan, one of the lowest in first-century society, attending to a wounded man lying in a gutter after a priest and a Levite, highly respected members of society and part of the clergy elite, had passed him by. The Samaritan brings the man to an inn and tells the proprietor to look after him, promising to reimburse the proprietor for all expenses. Who is the man of God? Jesus asks. It is the Samaritan, despite his lowly station.

When we consider the Samaritan's action, we see the connection between loving God and loving our neighbor. We can be sure that as the Samaritan man considered what he "ought" to do, his strong sense of morality strengthening him to help the man lying on the side of the road. This morality created the courage to act. An act that did not just extend to helping the injured man to an inn, but to offering to pay for all his expenses until he recovered. In doing this act, the Samaritan treated the neighbor as he himself would have liked to be treated. He also showed a relationship with God that respected the moral values that God wants us to embrace.

One of the great misconceptions about Jesus's view on morality is the belief that we should all be poor. Historical evidence tells us that Jesus earned an average living as a marketplace worker. How else would he have helped pay his family's bills? Jesus didn't say that making money was bad, but rather that you shouldn't make money at the expense of your neighbor, or against the will of God.

In a scene that is in all four of the Gospels, Jesus enters the temple of Jerusalem with a few friends and begins to turn over the tables of the money changers. He then turns to those selling the livestock used to make a sacrifice to God, and released the animals. He defiantly said, ***"Take these things out of here! Stop making my Father's house a marketplace!"*** (John 2:16)

As we look closer at Jesus's actions, we see a very close connection to his moral creed, "Love thy God and love thy neighbor." In the first-century Judean world, the temple was not only a center of the Jewish faith but it had also become a center of power and commerce. Those in power had turned the mighty temple into a money-making machine by taking advantage of the faithful Jewish population.

In the first century there were three critical festivals or holy periods observed in and around the temple, people from near and far came to honor God. The first was Pesach or, to us in English, Passover. The second, Sukkot or the Feast of the Tabernacles, marked the end of the harvest period and was an acknowledgment of the dependence on God. The third was called Shavout or Festival of Weeks, and occurred in midspring to celebrate the revelation of the Torah, the first five books of the Jewish Bible.

Much of the countryside came to make donations and sacrifices during these holy periods. The dominant currency of the Judean world was the Roman denar, on which the Roman emperor was depicted. Roman emperors considered themselves gods, which went against the monotheistic Jewish faith. As such, a denar could not be used for sacrificial donations. So tables were set up in the temple to allow the pilgrims to convert their denari into sacred shekels. The money changers then took advantage of this requirement and charged the worshippers excessive amounts to make the exchange, while often using rigged scales.

It was also common to make sacrifices of livestock during these periods, but not all who worshipped owned livestock and others had traveled from too far away to bring animals with them. So, at the temple, booths were set up to sell livestock. As you would guess, the livestock was sold at prices well above market value, but also, after the livestock was sacrificed, the meat was sold in the open markets outside the temple, making even more money for the power mongers. Additionally, each vendor was required to pay a franchise fee to those who ran the temple.

Jesus's actions put him in direct conflict with those who ran the temple and took advantage of their neighbors. Jesus was cutting off their money supply. This was a very dangerous thing to do, and in turn almost all scholars believe that his action of temple cleansing directly led to Jesus's crucifixion.

As a former worker and business owner who visited the temple, Jesus knew the system well. He also knew that it defied the principles of "love thy God and love thy neighbor." Jesus saw two abuses in these practices. For one, he saw merchants not honoring God and turning the temple into a place that defiled God. Secondly, he saw a faithful population being taken advantage of by their neighbors.

Why would the money changers and livestock sellers comply with the powerful who ran the temple? Why would they use commercial practices to defile God and take advantage of their neighbors? It is a simple answer that illustrates the human condition: They had to make a living in order to pay their bills. Over time, they came to compromise the values of God in order to live. Over time, the lure of money swamped their inner desire to be good. Over time, they moved away from where they wanted to be.

Before we judge them, we should consider our own marketplace. We, too, need to make money to pay our bills, but we also have worldly desires to increase our net worth for its own sake and gain favor with those in power. It is these desires that can move us from our right relationship with God and our neighbor to a struggle with temptation, the temptation to follow a path we know we should not take.

The apostle Paul describes this decision point in the Book of Romans by saying, ***"I do not understand my own actions. For I do not do what I want, but I do the very thing I hate."*** (Romans 7:15) It is a quandary all of us have found ourselves in at one time or another, because we, like Paul, are not perfect. Only Jesus is perfect, and many theologians believe that our imperfections are simply his way of teaching us God's values.

Jesus knows this dilemma and knows it well. He worked with those from the ancient marketplace and he works with us today. The answer to Paul's confusion doesn't rest within our internal struggle, but with the modeling of Jesus. Jesus asks us to rise above the natural desires of our human condition. Jesus asks us to act for God and our neighbor, which is at first a difficult road that requires courage, and many times a supplanting of our wishes. But it is a road that when followed leads us to a strengthened feeling of self-worth.

Most of us need to work in the marketplace. And if what we are asked to do in the marketplace is immoral, how can we remain moral ourselves and follow the lessons of Jesus?

The easiest answer is to quit. We took the job in the first place for earthly reasons. We wanted to care for our family, but personal ambition may also have prevailed: We wanted to buy things for ourselves, to use our job as a sign of social status. Walking away might make us feel good morally, but the paychecks will stop, our reputation may slip, we may become a "bad risk." All the material things we've been accustomed to may disappear. No wonder we are tempted to agree to insert a small mistake into the spreadsheet so our future looks better on paper. If our cigarettes contain nicotine, so what if we allege they're non-addictive?

But should our self-worth be based on material achievement? Jesus's ministry was in the marketplace not to prevent people from earning money for their family, but to change how they determined their self-worth: through kindness to their neighbor and a faithful obedience to God rather than monetary gain.

Jesus teaches us that taking the long road is actually shorter, which means we may have to stand up to the CEO, supervisor, or maybe even the board. It's not a question of *whether* to do it, it's a question of *when and how* to act. Always with love for the other, including the CEO. But Jesus asks us to act. You might get fired. You might have to wait for a long time to get a comparable job. You might have to make sacrifices, and so might your family. But the penalties for doing what's right are almost always impermanent; the rewards will last a lifetime. Sherron Watkins of Enron acted and survived and became *Time* magazine's Person of the Year.

The consequences, in other words, might not be as bad as you imagine. In 1999, I was promoted to be the new chief financial officer at Foot Locker. I was thrilled. True, the company was in terrible financial shape and in real danger of going under, but I was CFO for a Fortune 500 company, a publicly held company, and all I had to do was save it. I was forty-five years old and a life dream was being fulfilled.

Dear God, I had no idea what I was doing! I had some prior experience in financial management, I was a whiz at numbers, and I had my brains and many trusted friends who could give me advice, but I was adrift.

It was immediately obvious that we had to raise cash. The best way was to sell assets that were valuable but not related to Foot Locker's strategic plan. An asset that met these criteria was a retail chain called Afterthoughts that sold trinkets, such as charms, bracelets, and rings, to teenagers. Those of us in the finance department got our then-boss, Roger Farah, the CEO, to agree, and the corporate board backed us.

At my level in the company was our long-standing vice president for corporate development, a fancy name for an internal investment banker, who knew "just the right buyer." He wanted to sell Afterthoughts for two times EBITDA (earnings before income, taxes, depreciation, amortization—or the total cash the business generated). Roger was putting pressure on him to come up with cash in a hurry and this was the quickest way for him to assure income (and to look good to the CEO).

However, standard industry practice is to sell large subsidiary companies for six to ten times EBITDA. Thus the potential buyer of Afterthoughts was going to get a huge bargain in return for his cash. The company treasurer, John Cannon, called me to announce what was being recommended. John and others were very clear with me that I had to act. I was surrounded by highly moral associates looking for me to stand up. They all knew that what was happening was wrong, and they pushed me to do the right thing. *Oh boy,* I said to myself, and went over to the VP corporate development's office to object to the plan.

From outside his door, I could hear him screaming at his wife over the phone; his tone was harsh, demeaning, abusive. I knew I was in for a difficult conversation. I was in a quandary; on the one hand, I had John Cannon and others encouraging me to do the right thing, and on the other hand, I had a career-threatening task in front of me. Encouraged by a number of other people, I pushed forward. This encouragement by others pushed me to do what I didn't *want* to do, but knew I *had* to do.

"We have to sell Afterthoughts for seven times EBITDA," I told the VP when he had hung up.

"You're an idiot," he said. "What do you know? You're brand-new here. Don't you understand the pressure we're under?"

I nervously apologized. "Sorry. The banks won't let you sell at that price." At that point, the banks had as much say over Foot Locker as the CEO did.

His eyes blazed. "You were promoted to control the banks!"

"The banks will have done the numbers and won't agree with you," I explained. "They're not going to let you sell the company at two times EBITDA."

"We'll see about that," he growled, and marched off to Farah's office.

Roger came to see me. "What's going on here?" he asked angrily.

Knowing I had no other choice, I explained. "Roger, John Cannon and our treasury people have done the research. The banks won't let you sell the subsidiary at the current offer. Besides, we can get our price if we hold out for a little while. Why would we give away two hundred million dollars?"

Roger eventually agreed with me, and we finally sold the subsidiary for over $250 million. The vice president of corporate development remained my enemy while he was employed at Foot Locker, doing what he could to undermine me. The man eventually left within the year and I was safe for the moment.

What if I had let him get his way? I'd have been an accessory to a bad business decision that would have undermined the integrity of the company and the people who worked there. I would also have let down all those people who had encouraged me to speak up. In the end, I felt like I really had only one choice, but after our fight I realized what grave danger I'd been in along the way, of doing the wrong thing. The truth is I didn't know what I was doing, and so I just acted on instinct, and the encouragement of honest and faithful people.

From then on, I was on my guard, expecting the VP to try to get me fired, or move me out of the way in some other fashion. He had underestimated me and those advising me. My decision to hold out might have hurt the company temporarily and ended my career at Foot Locker, but it still was the right decision, and I quickly realized that this kind of tough decision had to be made every week, if not every day or hour, in the business world. Jesus and my neighbors from the company had helped me this time in ways I didn't understand. It would take years before I understood Jesus's teachings and how important he was in my life, but after I learned to listen to Jesus and to adopt his morality, similar decisions became easier and easier, and I showed more and more courage in making them.

I am of a belief that not all my Christian brothers and sisters share: that almost all people want to do and be good. But temptation confronts us and prevents us from being the people we want to be. *Go along. Avoid confronting those in power. Take the easy way. It's the CEO's responsibility.* The temptation trap is powerful, alluring, sometimes addictive. When we give in, we become unsettled. Augustine says that "our hearts are unquiet until they rest with the Lord." The struggle to follow Jesus is a difficult one. But it must be faced—and won.

One phase of business where it's tempting to cheat is in quarterly reporting. A friend who works in publishing describes being forced to put out a novel by a bestselling author before the book was ready to go to press. His firm needed a good end-of-the-year quarter, and the book could be on sale in November at the height of the holiday season, and those figures could be reported at year's end. The company would make its budget; sacrificed would be the quality of the book, which could have used another three months of rewriting.

My friend was the editor in chief. He howled to his boss, to the head of the parent company, but all to no avail. The author, already exhausted, was relieved not to have to work further. The upshot? The book was published three months too early, in the wrong quarter. It didn't sell as well as predicted and my friend lost his job.

While I was CFO at Foot Locker, thanks to the hard work of many people we made our budgeted figure in every quarter—in itself, something of a miracle. The banks were happy. Wall Street was happy. My boss, Roger Farah, was happy. We didn't do it by cooking the books, but by careful attention to costs, orders, and distribution. After each quarter, I would kick back with a beer and a sense of self-satisfaction, only to begin the next day by worrying about the quarter to come.

Wall Street investors visited regularly. "How are sales going?" they'd ask. We refused to answer this question. There is an SEC rule called Regulation FD—Fair Disclosure—meaning we could not selectively reveal any nonpublic information. In doing so, we would be giving one investor an unfair advantage over other potential investors. Thus, we did not provide interim updates unless all investors and potential investors received the information at the same time. I strongly agreed with the Securities and Exchange position, but was always amazed that at virtually every meeting, we were asked questions by investors the answers to which would put me and Foot Locker in violation of the regulation.

For example, they would almost always ask the question "Are you going to do a stock buyback?" Answering this question would not only violate Regulation FD, but it was also an answer that could weaken the company.

When your company buys back its own stock, it shows that the company has faith in itself. But there's a financial message as well. If you have a hundred shares outstanding, and you're making $100, you're earning a dollar a share. But if you buy back ten percent of the stock, the outstanding shares are now earning $1.10, and the stock price should go up by ten percent. Most corporations use this common ploy. And once you announce the buyback—you're required to make it public—your Wall Street investors can sell their holdings and make a ten percent profit. However, for a business still not an "investment grade" company, the buyback will weaken its credit standing and threaten its survival. The investors would come to our meetings, watch us carefully, and pounce if they noticed anything amiss. As in poker, body language was a "tell."

Most Wall Street investors are nice people, wonderful to be with at a dinner party or on a golf course. But at meetings such as the ones at Foot Locker, "nice" is not the word I'd use to describe them.

The main goal of businesses is to maximize profits; that's how things work in a capitalist society. It isn't a question of whether it's a noble goal, it's how you reach that goal that matters. Vince Lombardi, a deeply faithful Christian, is often quoted as saying, "Winning is the only thing," but what he actually said was "The spirit, the will to win and the will to excel—these are the things that endure and these are the qualities that are so much more important than any of the events that occasion them." In other words, you don't do *anything* to win, you don't cheat, but instead you always have a spirit to win.

The urge to bend the rules or produce inferior products in order to make higher profits is always present. Whether we're talking about a large auto company fudging its emissions standards or a first-century money changer rigging the scales. Temptation is always there. However, these gains are always short-term. The question is not if they will be discovered, but when they will be discovered. And when they are, the price to pay is many multiples larger than the short-term gain.

Jesus knows this, and through the parables of the marketplace he provides us the road map to model.

There are companies with the values of excellence, who put the product and customer first without subterfuge. Yankee Candle, where I worked after leaving Foot Locker, is a "clean" company, which is why ninety-three percent of their customers "passionately" like them, the highest brand rating by customers in America. L.L.Bean, the mail order clothing company, is also a good example of a business that puts quality and customer satisfaction first. Leonard L. Bean, its founder, had a simple philosophy: "Make a reasonable product, sell it at a reasonable price, make a reasonable profit." Leonard Bean is dead, but his successors have carried on his tradition. I know they've succeeded, and I'm still wearing the Bean clothes I bought when Leonard was alive, well over thirty years ago. When you call their customer service line, many times the call is answered on the first ring by a human voice. They are always friendly and courteous. L.L.Bean doesn't use slogans, it uses quality, to win over customers. They have a spirit of excellence, courageously driven by a high moral commitment to their neighbor. When we read the parables of Jesus designed for the marketplace, we see that same simple philosophy.

How do you, as a person from the marketplace who has been forced to compromise in order to keep your job, still maintain—and this is the best way I know to put it—your self-worth? Through a continuous relationship with God, centered around prayer.

Jesus wasn't resurrected to teach us religion; he came to bring us to a more personal relationship with God. God, through his Son, is in direct contact with us—but don't ask for his help in winning the lottery. Jesus and God are not genies, and we will always be disappointed in the response if this is how we approach the relationship, that our wish is their command. But if we make Jesus's teachings part of our lives and our self-worth, we begin to hear God's answer.

For those of us in the marketplace, we should start with daily meditation and prayer. I generally pray and meditate in the quiet of my yard before setting out in the morning, but the time and place aren't important; anytime and anywhere will do. For those of us learning to pray, Jesus gave us the Lord's Prayer. It contains all that's required: praise, petition, and rejoice. Simple but effective.

You see a problem. You ask yourself why the problem exists and what to do about it. You meditate and pray. God won't whisper in your ear, nor will he appear in the heavens above, but God *will* answer your prayer. We may see that answer in a set of coincidences over the next few days. Perhaps we will see it in a Bible verse that comes to our attention. It might happen through a discussion with a random person. Generally, I don't feel it is an answer unless I have three of these happenings and the answer is biblically sound. Then I know I have been heard. One day at Drew Theological School, I was approached by a fellow student and wonderful pastor, Wendy Paige. She told me about a number of strange occurrences of this sort that had happened recently in her life and wondered if the same thing ever happened to me.

"All the time," I assured her.

"How do we know it's from God and not a coincidence?"

Being a math and business person, I replied, "The laws of probability. If it occurs here and there, it may be a form of delusion. I look for three confirmations. Then it is probably God responding to my prayers."

"You use math to find God..." Wendy replied.

"I do, it is my language."

Over the years I have had many discussions with faithful people who reply in a similar way.

13

Are these coincidences or real answers? If they are unusual and better than what you hoped for and occur frequently, then they are probably genuine answers.

God's answers always come in an unusual way; they don't happen every day or every time you ask. But you will know when it is God answering your prayer. The prophet Elijah experienced his answers as a gentle wind.

Ignatius of Loyola, the great Jesuit, stressed the importance of prayer mainly because the response to prayer builds faith. Years after I left Yankee Candle, I was approached by two headhunters with offers of work at large companies. I prayed and asked for guidance. I think God told me to continue what I was doing; to use what I'd learned from Jesus to help others in the marketplace. Notice I use the word "think"; I'm not sure. However, previous attempts to re-enter corporate life had ended in dissatisfaction and failure, and my prayers of what to do this time, I felt, were answered with a strong no.

Lately, a sense of joy occurred for me after moving beyond these temptations. I refused both offers at great financial cost, turning instead to writing this book, and continuing my activities as a servant-leader, helping those whose homes were destroyed by super-storm Sandy, helping inner city youths gain access to higher education, organizing a trip to Africa to help the orphans of parents afflicted by AIDS, serving on the board of a Phi Beta Kappa college, helping build a maternity ward in Haiti, studying to receive my doctorate degree in ministry, and answering calls of help from former business acquaintances.

Did I make the right choice? Business had been my life, my passion; my hands itched to expand my résumé. I thought of the costs of sending our four children to college, of making the needed repairs to our house, of giving my wife, Connie, every comfort she deserves. The temptations were powerful, but my faith told me I had to continue serving Jesus, humankind, and the marketplace, and that's the path I'm following. I'm not looking for respect from my readers; no "good man" from them is necessary. God, through Jesus, told me what to do.

What good is faith when your boss tells you, "We're not making the numbers?" I'll soon introduce you to several people faced with this dilemma, and for many, standing up for the truth was, in the short run, a tough decision. In the long run—well, that's what this book is about.

A woman named Lauren Peters, now in her fifties, worked for me for many years, almost always as the second in charge, and certainly hugely influential in my life. She fought most of her battles with a strong and courageous Christian faith, many times having to reveal results that were potentially harmful to the company, and certainly not what the company desired, but she was unafraid, and I believe it was her bravery and faith that kept her at the firm—and at my side.

In 2004, Foot Locker had a chance to buy out its chief competitor, Footaction. I negotiated the deal with the help of then-CEO of Foot Locker, Matt Serra. The board was happy: After all, we were about to buy out our chief competitor. I brought in Lauren to do a final due diligence, and she soon discovered that Footaction was subtly cooking their books. It was her duty to tell me. She knew how happy I was about the deal, knew that I'd have to go back to Matt and the board and tell them we shouldn't buy the company until the discrepancies were resolved, and that Footaction and its parent, Meldisco, would likely have to file for bankruptcy. She knew she'd have to face the most rigorous questioning. But still, she came to me with a deep-rooted faith and a strong moral compass, and asked that I listen to her. In the end everyone agreed with Lauren's assessment and pulled out of the deal. Later, Footaction's parent did file for bankruptcy. However, after resolving the legal issues associated with a bankruptcy, we purchased Footaction for a fraction of the originally agreed-upon price.

In the marketplace, Jesus teaches us that courageous faith and morality, centered on God and our neighbor, are more important than spreadsheets, projections, or due diligence. Faith without morality isn't true faith, but Lauren had both. There was no way we could go ahead with that purchase, dealing with an unethical partner. In a different company, under a different CEO, Lauren might have been axed or ignored. Today, she's CFO for Foot Locker, and one of the most respected retail CFOs in America.

We are faced every day with decisions that can have far-reaching consequences. We are tempted in the marketplace at almost every corner and we struggle with what to do next. Herein lies the value of Jesus in our marketplace lives. His teachings, ways, and words can help guide us, making our paths straighter and helping us to avoid those events and decisions that can create crippling consequences.

CHAPTER 2

THE CALLING

"Worship the Lord your God, and serve only him."

–MATTHEW 4:10

When I was in college at Suffolk University in Boston during the early 1970s, there were eight major public accounting firms—the "Big Eight"—Haskins & Sells among them. If you saw a future career in finance, as I did, you usually had one of three choices: You could work for a mom-and-pop CPA business, or a medium-sized firm, or you had the goal of getting a job with one of the Big Eight. As a junior in college I was able to land a job with one of those big firms, Haskins & Sells, now called Deloitte Touche Tohmatsu, and there I started to learn my craft. For many of us, accounting wasn't looked at as a career in those days, but as a stepping-stone to a life in business, a way of paying your dues. For me, though, the title of CFO had a majesty to it.

I was fast and accurate—head-scratchers were my specialty—so I was drawn to any aspect of the business that involved creating solutions, creating profits in particular. My dream of being a CFO meant

I would have to be adept at looking for innovative ways to make and save money for the company, being second in command to the chief executive officer—the nuts-and-bolts man rather than the visionary. The rise up this ladder is from assistant controller to controller and then to CFO, similar to a baseball player's rise from A-Ball to Triple-A to the major leagues.

While a CFO is well paid, being rich was not my ambition; success in business itself was. I wanted to be in "The Show." My goal was to be CFO at a Fortune 500 company, something like Apple, Exxon, or Nike, which would put me in an elite class. By definition, there are only five hundred such CFOs in the world, and they comprise the pantheon.

My first major job was as an assistant divisional controller at a May Department Stores division in Connecticut. May was then a prestigious, nationwide Fortune 500 company. It was there that I rose from divisional assistant controller to divisional CFO in seven years, but I was still not a corporate CFO.

Foot Locker asked me to join them and I was elated, not only because it was another Fortune 500 company, but because the job was as corporate controller, a person who dealt personally with the Securities and Exchange Commission, with all the responsibility that description implies.

The journey from division CFO to corporate controller at a Fortune 500 company is an arduous one, and moral pitfalls abound. At Foot Locker, I was given the additional responsibility of a facility they owned in Harrisburg, Pennsylvania. The facility housed all the back office functions for Foot Locker, such as accounts payable, data processing, accounting, and so forth. When I first arrived there, I noticed that there was no solicitation from the employees of ideas about how to do things better. Instead, the building had a number of consultants telling management what to do. From my past, I knew that hidden in the minds of the rank and file there were better opinions. So, with the help of a very open and thoughtful executive who worked for me, Mike Zawosky, using a method I had helped developed many years earlier, we began a process of soliciting ideas from the people that did those jobs every day. The process was very simple: Mike would circulate the building and talk to employees, developing their ideas. We then held a monthly meeting where the employees gave us their ideas and we would reward them with money, trips, or tickets to major sporting events. The first few months we did this the process was met with overwhelming success, the company experiencing $5 million in expense reductions that increased profits. We'd paid out five hundred thousand dollars in rewards.

When the folks at corporate headquarters heard about this program, it was met with strong disapproval. The consultants were costing us significantly more than the incentives we'd paid to the employees, and had delivered no savings. I was surprised at the push-back from the higher-ups.

A senior member of HR called me one day and said, "I heard you paid out a lot of money to the employees with this new program you set up. The consultants are very upset."

"True," I said. "However, the company improved its earnings by almost five million dollars and morale is soaring because people are being listened to."

Silence at the other end.

"Why is this a problem?" I asked, already anticipating the answer. "Earnings are up because of this process."

The fellow on the other end of the line hesitated. Finally, he said, "The consultants think you're stepping on their turf."

I calmly stated, "The consultants haven't found any money to help us, but their bills each month keep getting paid. I think they should be sent home."

"You can't fire them, they are well liked by a number of us," I was warned.

"Okay, I'll give them thirty days to show value or we have to let them go," I offered, positive they were not going to help the company.

My colleague agreed to the schedule, the consultants didn't show value, and I released them. The process that Mike and I had started grew and contributed significantly to the earnings of the company. I was named Employee of the Year and still keep the memento as a reminder of the importance of listening and of persevering.

The same incentive program still exists today and annually contributes tens of millions of dollars to Foot Locker's bottom line. Employees are still rewarded with money, trips to Disney World, Super Bowls, and so on.

Don't get me wrong about consultants; they can provide benefit to companies, but they must be paid based on results. That year at Foot Locker, we paid our consultants $75 million, with very few tangible results. People do what you pay them to do, not what you ask them to do.

The issue of paying for friends of some members of the company, friends who weren't contributing, versus rewarding employees for going beyond their jobs to help, was difficult to overcome. But thanks to an open-minded CEO and the production of positive results, we all survived.

Another event happened early on that also produced a dangerous situation: One of the many retail chains we owned was called Woolworth's. Woolworth's was a billion-dollar division and, at one time, the biggest retail operation in America, before the advent of Walmart. Normal retail standards and generally accepted accounting principles required an inventory of our assets.

I looked at the Woolworth's inventory we were about to announce. Uh-oh! Dead parakeets were in the inventory, right out of a Monty Python sketch. Shoes where one of the pair was defective were included. Products marked "out of stock" were there as well. I removed the questionable items from the list, cutting the "worth" of our inventory by $100 million. It was then up to me to tell the division head and the CEO about the shortfall, not a pleasant prospect.

He exploded. "You're only submitting this inventory to make your bonus better for next year, right?" He was implying that I was trying to make the present year look bad so it would look better under my watch the year after.

I didn't think so, and didn't rescind the figures. Roger Farah, the Foot Locker CEO, called. "They're saying you screwed up the inventory on purpose," he said.

"I'm not counting dead parakeets *on purpose*?" I asked incredulously.

Most corporate CEOs have to deal with he-said-she-said, and Roger had only my word against years of false accounting practice. I was in a really bad position, worried about keeping my job, but I stood my ground.

Roger, being Roger, ended up agreeing with me. He told all relevant employees that what I said went, and we booked the appropriate adjustment to our inventory value.

While I had done the right thing morally, it was because I was adapting lessons learned earlier in life from other places I had worked. While Connie and I attended church on a regular basis, I wasn't yet aware of the full impact Jesus would have on my life. Only later would I understand that I had taken the narrow gate that Jesus had stated was the best and hardest way.

I had saved the company from embarrassment, I felt, since the inventory discrepancies were sure to have been discovered. My head swelled. It was at this point that I started to lose my humility and begin a slow descent. As I became more successful, I also became more prideful. If you go to my LinkedIn profile, you'll see that Bruce

Hartman was indeed responsible for saving the company; a number of people who worked for me posted it there.

But it's not true. Now I believe—I'm positive—that it was really God who was responsible; not by having me hired, but because God surrounded me with good, moral, profoundly honest people like Lauren, Mike, Peter B., Marc, Peter C., Joe, Kevin, and many others who did the grunt work and picked the company up. They held the goal line in what appeared sometimes to be a futile cause. True, I put them in a position to rescue the company, and I pushed them hard. But like a football coach, I didn't throw the pass, didn't score the touchdown, didn't make the saving tackle; I simply told them what needed to be done. These people had faith, strong ethics, and a desire to succeed. I didn't realize it then, but I realize it now. I succeeded because of these great people and Jesus.

The day I was made CFO at Foot Locker in 1999, its stock sold for a historically low three dollars a share. Over time, I amassed thousands of stock options, and as the stock price went up, so did my net worth. One day, thinking I had enough to take care of my family, particularly my girls' education, I decided to sell my stock, every share of it. I hadn't lost faith in the company, quite the contrary, and probabilities were that if I kept the stock it would increase in value, but I wanted to be sure I had enough money for my family, and retail is a dangerous, inherently cyclical business.

When an officer of a publicly held company decides to sell his stock, it can be a sign he thinks the company is in trouble, and technically he has to announce his misgivings. Trouble didn't exist in my case, but the sale wouldn't look good to the outside world. Both the board and the new CEO of Foot Locker, Matt Serra, were furious. However, I came from a very modest background and this was a chance to solidify my family's security. My financial advisor told me to sell. I hadn't lost faith in the company, but they had in me, and eventually I was fired in 2005.

After leaving Foot Locker, I began to get stirrings. Stirrings to change my life direction. I felt that these were coming from God. I noticed unusual events in my thoughts and actions. For instance, when good things happened, I found myself thanking God. Thanking God for the beauty of the things in life. I also started getting encouragement from my pastor to consider a different path. I began considering going to school to learn more about Jesus. I had the money and time. Later, as I looked back on this period, I felt that God was telling me, *You have done what you set out to do. Your family is safe and you are where you wanted to be. It's now time to turn to me, your God.*

I ignored this push and continued to see my self-worth in terms of my ability to generate money. I went to work for Cushman & Wakefield, the premier commercial real estate firm in the world. I was their executive vice president and CFO. I had always admired Cushman, because of the way they did business. When I was at Foot Locker we thought of expanding to China, like everyone else. The representatives of Cushman could have made a lot of money from this expansion, but they advised against the move. Their analysis was that with a sliding scale on rents we would never make money. In other words, as we grew the rent would increase, as was the custom in China. Even though we were a Fortune 500 company, we weren't big enough to get flat rent deals.

During my interviews prior to taking the job at Cushman, I saw this same commitment to the customer through Bruce Mosler and John Santora, the CEO and COO. Bruce, in particular, was very impressive. He was the consummate deal maker and had a heart for doing the right thing for Cushman and his customers. Bruce was brilliant in his thoughts, but prone to being explosive.

My favorite story about Bruce was the day Donald Trump called his office when we were working on an important strategy for the company. Bruce's secretary came in to the meeting and announced, "Mr. Trump is on the phone and is very firm about wanting to talk to you."

Bruce stated, "Tell him I'm busy and will call him back."

I said, "Bruce, you know that was Donald Trump on the phone?"

"He's important, but what we are working on is more important," he explained.

I remember thinking, *He really does care about being a great CEO.*

After my first week on the job, Bruce came into my office and said, "I'm going to try to sell the company or file for an IPO."

Wow, this was going to be short-lived job, I said to myself. I knew that filing for an IPO was inherently not in the cards, because 30 percent ownership was split among the brokers, Bruce, and other employees; they would not agree to an eighteen-month lockup of their stock.

Generally, when a company files an IPO, the investment bankers require that all existing management that owns stock keep their stock for an extended period of time. This is called a lockup period. It is important because it helps ensure that the company doesn't fudge the numbers before the IPO filing. So if a sale to another company was likely, my job was to maximize the value for all the shareholders, and an IPO would not accomplish this task.

We also were owned by the Rockefeller Group, the owners of Rockefeller Center, who in turn were owned by a Japanese company called Mitsubishi Estate. The combination of these two cultures was not compatible with a commercial real estate firm, and this was consistently obvious. Our owners were both very conservative and not used to the flamboyant ways of real estate. There was constant tension. For instance, ownership insisted we address them as Mr. This or That, but they would only refer to us by our first names. My solution was to address them always as they addressed me, by first name. This raised eyebrows and created some conflict, but my conclusion was that we would be sold anyway and I should focus on that.

By the end of the year, we were indeed sold, to an Italian company. It was clear to me that these two cultures wouldn't mesh either and that I should consider leaving. The financial oversight from our new owners was stifling and mostly inappropriate. For example, after many hours of negotiations, we put together a typical American bank deal. I was sure they would be happy, but in fact they felt that they had a bad deal. Their concern was that if they didn't have the money to pay the banks back, they didn't want to use assets to pay them back. I protested that when people loan you money, they have a right to be paid back. After many discussions, they relented, but a level of distrust toward me developed.

After the sale was completed, I told Bruce that while I enjoyed working for him, I didn't feel comfortable with the new owners. He pushed me hard and I agreed to give it one year. After six months I knew it wasn't a fit and I began to look elsewhere.

During this period, I was approached by Yankee Candle to be their CFO. I was very impressed with the CEO, Craig Ryden, and the COO, Harlan Kent. I felt their brand and commitment to excellence were extraordinary. They were people with values of decency and fair play. After two years of turmoil it would be a place of refuge for me. So I left Cushman and again went to work at a new company.

I had earned a sizeable amount of money from Cushman, as I had bought into the company. The company was sold after a doubling of its earnings, some of which was greatly aided by our expense initiatives. Getting the money from the new owners, as you would guess, took a considerable amount of effort, including the threat of legal action.

I continued to get the stirrings. It was only later, through my reading of the Bible, that I realized this latest employment move of mine was Jesus again "knocking on my door."

Craig Ryden was the best CEO of the many great ones I worked for. He was unfailingly polite, friendly, compassionate; the only time I saw him rattled was during the market crash in 2008.

Jesus would have approved of him. To Craig, the customer really did come first, and he thought about the quality of the product more than short-term profits. This attention to fair play and product quality in turn led to a more sustainable sales-and-profit picture for the future. He was so pro-employee that you could make the argument he favored workers over the company. He was from a small town in New Hampshire, and the positive qualities of coming from a small, closely knit community showed up every day.

I was happy at Yankee Candle, but I was under both internal and external pressure to turn closer toward God. Our family had moved to New Jersey and was attending the United Methodist Church. Its pastor, Paul Maliel, knowing my dissatisfaction with the business world and the state of my heart, continued to talk to me about attending theological school.

I had grown up in a religious household and prayer had always been part of my life. Jesus, to me, was your traditional Sunday school image. I made the sign of the cross habitually, a reaction that meant little except "thanks" when good things happened. To me, Jesus was an abstract figure with a halo, romanticized not only in art and legend, but in the icons, postcards, and statues I saw around me. Connie and I were decent followers on Sundays, although I would too often let golf get in the way. I didn't question God's existence, or the power of his Son, but I didn't really pay much attention to Jesus's teachings.

Over time, even in quiet moments alone, I found I couldn't pray. I had *forgotten* how to pray! It was the lowest point in my life. I was far removed where I wanted to be as a human being. Sadly, I had learned to measure myself by my material possessions.

One cool spring morning in 2009, I was restless and couldn't get back to sleep, so I decided to take a walk. The more I walked, the more distressed I became. Finally, almost home, I approached a crack in the sidewalk and noticed the way the light hit it; darkness behind the crack and light ahead. It was at that moment that I realized I no longer had a connection with God. Most of what I'd hoped for in my youth, in a spiritual sense, was missing. I was selfish, prone to anger, impatient, lustful, and generally believed I could do no wrong. Soon after this event, I started to keep a diary, and in it I referred to myself as "Mr. Big." However, I wasn't Mr. Big, but Mr. Small. Overwhelming grief filled me. My heart was restless. I tried to pray and was convinced I had failed. Had I lost God forever?

My brother-in-law, Kenny, is a minister and I called him.

"I knew you were going to call," he claimed. From a distance he had watched my slow descent.

I described to him what was happening in my life. His heart was touched by my dilemma, and to my intense relief, he was open with me, and sympathetic. Through this conversation I felt as though God had answered my prayer.

Kenny sent me a reading from the Bible. I found it drew me into an old familiar place, the Bible itself. I was compelled to read Matthew 4:1–11, regarding the temptation of Christ. I was not sure why I was compelled to read these verses, other than the fact that I felt the spirit tell me this was a place to start. In this passage, I found three important points. The first was *"One does not live by bread alone, but by every word that comes from the mouth of God."* (Matthew 4:4) For me, this meant that I must turn to God and move away from being a materialistic predator. The second was *"Do not put the Lord your God to the test."* (Matthew 4:7) In other words, I needed to begin answering the stirrings that had started years ago. The third and most important to me at that time was ***"Worship the Lord your God, and serve only him."*** (Matthew 4:10) After an extended period of habitually acquiring material possessions, it was time to serve God. These three verses may sound easy to comply with, but for me, after a lifetime of moving away from God, they indicated a radically different path. At this point, I was unaware of the difficulty of following these three principles and that I wouldn't just achieve this new life because I wanted to, but that it would become a daily struggle.

On the third day, after reflection and almost continuous Bible reading, I went for a late evening walk to a bench that was to become an important prayer spot. It was on this bench on that night that I prayed I could listen to the words of Jesus and become committed to following his way. Each time I said, "I will only follow the words of Jesus," I was met with thoughts of what I would have to give up; for me it was overwhelming.

This inner battle went on for an extended time that evening, and I felt physically removed from the debate. It was as if I had drifted into the sky and was watching the fight for my soul from above.

I left the bench and felt the relief of knowing I'd be able to resist the pull of the advantages a material life could offer. It was from this point that I began to chart an alternative way of thinking. I left Yankee Candle and began the difficult road to a different life.

I immersed myself in rediscovering God. I now believed I had to go to theological school; there was one at Drew University, a short distance from my house. A lot of good Christians get their answers by going to church, but I felt I had to know more.

I entered Drew Theological School with the goal of getting a Master's in Divinity. Immediately, I was overwhelmed. The complexity of theological thought was foreign to a person who had spent most of his life in business. For the first year, my life was in a period of deconstruction. The professors rid all of us students of our precon-ceived ideas, learned from a life of not really being connected to the Bible and being instead under the influence of contemporary thought. We were also pressed to think critically and formulate our own thoughts. We all had to erase our past and reenter the Bible without the comfort of what we had previously learned.

During this process, I began to observe a number of things. Theological thought was both doctrinal and deeply personal. The dis-cussions we had exposed a wide range of views and many different ways to think about God. These views, driven by each individual's past, created different lenses on how to reenter the Bible. Over time, I began to move away from the dogma of doctrine and toward a simple theology: love our God and love my neighbor. Issues of pre-destined lives, creationism, and was there a snake in the garden became less important, now replaced by how to live and help others live the sev-en-word theology of *Love our God and love my neighbor*.

I also began to notice how marketplace workers, a group consid-ered to be the root of wrongs in our world, were missing from these discussions. The presence of a few of us from the marketplace was tol-erated, but our ideas were not readily accepted. We talked a different language. We focused on getting things done. We were not attracted to lengthy discourse. We were simpler in our views. We got to the point quickly, after years of training to approach life productively.

I also noticed this approach consistently in Jesus. Jesus used simple words and parables to reveal God's message. Jesus spent most of his time not with the religious elite but with the everyday men and women from the first-century marketplace. Jesus didn't use polysyl-labic words. His message was for the heart and to be easily understood. He was for every person and from the marketplace himself. It was here in these thoughts that I realized that Jesus was pro-worker and that most of his messages were for the marketplace. A unique connection missed by many, including the professors for whom I developed a great deal of respect.

My two favorite theologians became Dietrich Bonhoeffer and Karl Barth, both tempered by the Holocaust, both believing that religion was a creation of man, an idea with which I agreed. There are, I think, profound differences in how we think about Jesus. But Jesus didn't invent Methodism or Catholicism, his purpose was the revelation of God. I also liked these two theologians because my conservative friends considered them too liberal and my liberal friends considered them too conservative. They were rational, relative, and right in the middle.

I noticed as well that the politics of morality in the church were no worse than they were in corporate life. Like people in most corporate cultures, most clergy were sincere in their efforts, but they were subject to the same temptations I had found in the business world, and I had to be careful with the leaders. Some leaders were good, but some used backstabbing, chicanery, ambition, and ruthlessness to impose their will. As in the corporate world, we had to be wary. Power can be very corrupting, but one's relation to God and his Son are pure, unambiguous—holy.

In learning the process of Biblical deconstruction, removing preconceived ideas, and using critical thinking, a reframing occurred for me regarding the Bible verses and my Sunday school instruction. I saw that the value was more in the message of God and less in the biblical history.

For instance, many scholars think that the Old Testament (more appropriately known as the Jewish Bible) was written by five groups of authors who were inspired by God. One group is called the Elohists. Similar to Aesop, they were storytellers. Since only five percent of the population could read and write in ancient times, both Testaments are made up of interesting stories that were passed along verbally, much like the parables that Jesus taught. To understand what God means, you must interpret the stories.

Personally, I agree that the Bible was written by people inspired by God. The Bible is therefore an accurate reflection of God's desire. However, because of cultural and individual life circumstances, it speaks to each person differently.

To a child, the story of the tortoise and the hare is a tale about running a race. But to an adult, it teaches a lesson: The faster you go, the worse the outcome. Stories in the Bible add a depth that allows people to enter from a familiar spot, their own life experience. But they also raise questions. Was there actually a snake in a Garden of Eden? If so, could it talk? Literalists will say there really was a talking snake. But there are those who view the Bible as metaphorical and will say no, it's a story to show God's way. Both could be right, but to me, it doesn't matter. For me, it is the lesson of morality and the authority of the Bible that matter. In this story, the message is that the snake is the voice of evil, Satan's voice, and to listen to it is dangerous, perhaps fatal.

The Bible also tells us the story of the Samaritan woman who meets Jesus at a well at noontime. He finds she is an outcast, a wanton woman who may have been married five times and is presently living with a man who is not her husband. Jesus takes pity on her and convinces her to convert her entire community to Christianity.

But wait a moment. A scholar might tell you that this story didn't happen. For one thing, a single man did not talk to a single woman during the first century, let alone a Jew talking to a Samaritan. For another, what would a Middle Eastern woman be doing going out in the 120-degree heat of the day to get water? Why not early morning when the work would be cooler? Again, these questions don't eliminate the realness of the message. They add texture to the story. They allow others to enter the story from their own life perspective. The story is still about the holiness of the lowest of the low, a castoff, and the power of the teachings of Jesus to change the world.

During this time, I met a pastor named Rich Teeters. He spoke simply and clearly. When I listened to his sermons, I always felt he was speaking directly to me. He knew how to make each of us listening to his sermons feel this way. But he was flawed. Unlike some who retreated from their flaws, he recognized his imperfections. His flaws exposed his humanity but made him accessible; we could identify with him. He didn't judge us. He was one of us. He was made in the image of God but knew he wasn't God. He taught me the humility needed to read and interpret the Bible. He insisted I stay open and nonjudgmental, allowing others to have their views.

At Drew, I also learned the danger of engaging in religious debate and retreated away when I saw these coming. My focus became simply "Love our God and love my neighbor." I learned to explore how Jesus works and who Jesus was. Those other debates led nowhere other than acrimony.

After three grueling years, I graduated in 2013 and was given the Daniel B Kidder Award for achieving the highest GPA in Pastoral Theology. I remember over the last few months at Drew looking at the incoming first-year students with their grand views and assured demeanor that they knew everything. I knew their personal journey was just beginning and that they would be changed by the time they graduated, as I was.

I spent three years at Drew Theological School and, because of my business experience, was asked to become something akin to the chief operating officer of the Methodist Church of New Jersey. I accepted instantly. The prospect of putting my skills toward working for God was heady and exciting. But it didn't work.

I didn't get fired or make any major mistakes, but before a year was out, I realized I couldn't go on. *This isn't right*, I told myself. We were a group of dedicated workers but little regard was paid to our well-being. We worked a full eight-hour day, followed by meetings at which the leaders of the church discussed the problems (many financial) we were facing.

At one late night meeting, the man who ran the library and our archives said he needed two thousand dollars for expansion. Most of our discussions concerned hundreds of thousands of dollars, not a few thousand, but on and on he droned, justifying his two grand. I had to leave the room twice because I was so irritated. When I came back the second time, he was still talking. I could see others fidgeting in their chairs. I noticed a woman, who for privacy reasons I will call Julia, getting very anxious. I knew she had two sick children at home and really needed to leave. "Okay, we hear your point," I told the library man impatiently. "Shouldn't we move on to the next subject?" To the Methodist leaders, only the workings of the church mattered. They wanted everyone to give up their home life for weekend retreats and late hours. In fact, over a ten-week period, I was asked to be away from my family more than I would be home. How different is that from a company that would resent my leaving early so I could visit my sick wife?

The man got his two thousand dollars. When the meeting finally ended, our chairperson, Vicki, pulled me aside and scolded me. "That wasn't very relational," she said.

"Our priorities are misdirected," I told her. "Julia was being forced to listen to him for sixty minutes, and she's got sick kids at home who need her. Who's not being relational? The guy made her uncomfortable, while these kids are without their mother, all to ask for two thousand dollars."

I've sat through dozens of business meetings where hours were wasted on puffery and self-importance. The fact that in this case the grandstanding "for the good of God" doesn't increase its relevancy. The rivalries within the church hierarchy are exactly the same as they can be in the boardroom.

Just as in the business world, the small betrayal, the petty ploy, the competitive stroke is often accompanied by a smile, a clap on the back, a tone of honey. Hypocrisy is a sin shared by both worlds. As one publishing executive told me, speaking of the charm of his British counterparts, "The English will cut you just as fiercely, but they put Novocain on the knife." I can't honestly tell you that there is any more humane sense in the church than there is in business.

On Sunday mornings, I used to help feed the poor, partly because I wanted to help a church at the Jersey Shore that needed to raise its attendance. I would walk down the streets of Bradley Beach and stop in at restaurants. If I saw that the restaurant displayed a cross, I would ask for a donation of food, and they would give it to us. "FREE BREAKFAST" read a sign on the church grounds, and I would man a table as the poor arrived. We started to get forty to fifty people in need every Sunday rather than the usual fifteen regular, mostly female attendees.

The women were offended that the poor had joined them. I remember being accosted one day by one of their sons. "You've ruined my mother's church," he declared.

"Your mother's church? She built it?"

He slunk away.

✝ ✝ ✝

One day, I had what I thought was an epiphany while I was on a long bike ride. My real calling, I decided, was not to help the church per se, but to help the business world. Jesus would be part of what I was trying to do, although I called my new company Gideon, after the famed trumpeter who brought the Israelites together on behalf of

God. I rationalized that my helping businesses out would be for the good of God.

The first year was a commercial success. I took ninety-eight airplane trips across the country to private equity firms, businesses of every kind, and even the Texas Methodist Foundation, which needed help in their business affairs. I advised on financial matters: when to pay bills; what expenses could logically be cut; how best to use a bank; how to interpret sales numbers. I was averaging about fifty thousand dollars a month.

Success, however, was no balm to my feeling that I wasn't serving Jesus. So I changed my focus. Instead of helping businesses prosper, I would help the individuals who made up those businesses, many of whom, including the highest placed executives, faced moral decisions every day. I reached out to them and it immediately felt good. I believed I would be able to help.

"How do I deal with my situation?" many asked. "How do I manage to stay at a job that I hate, but need in order to feed my family?" Follow Jesus or learn from Jesus's teachings are the simple answers, although it can be a journey to get there.

Today, I don't formally charge for my services, and when asked, I tell my clients to pay what they can afford and what they feel my time is worth to them. Many times I will unexpectedly receive a generous payment for my services, but my real payment is seeing people moving ahead with life.

As I look back on my life, like a lot of people, I wish that I knew then what I know now. I wish that I could have been there for friends in need. I was often too busy with my own life and too distant from the teachings of Jesus, and there were places where I could have helped if I'd known better.

Years before, when I worked for the May Company, one of the people who worked for me was a man named Randy Sanderson, an honest man with very high values. Randy, in turn, worked with another honest executive, Gerard Baja. After I left May, Randy was recruited by Dollar General to be their controller. Naturally, he took Gerard, another friend, with him. Things didn't turn out well for Gerard and Randy. Soon after, Gerard called me, asking for a job.

"What happened at Dollar General?" I asked, astonished.

He and Randy had been told to cook the books. "We shouldn't be doing this," Gerard said. "Randy, tell the CFO we refuse."

Randy advised his boss it was wrong, but the boss refused to listen. Fudging the books wasn't Randy's normal M.O., I knew, but in this instance, worried about his family, unwilling to look for a different job after he had so recently been hired, he gave in. Almost immediately, the company was investigated by the SEC. "We only did what we were supposed to do," Gerard and Randy said.

"No, you didn't," answered the SEC investigator. "You didn't call us."

In a public company, you not only work for that company, you work for its shareholders. If the shareholders are being cheated, the SEC has to be informed. Neither Randy nor Gerard had contacted the SEC, and the result was that these two honest men were barred from ever working again at a public company. It was like saying that both men would be working for half salary the rest of their lives.

At the time, I told Gerard that I sided with the SEC's viewpoint, that he and Randy had had an obligation to pick up the phone and call them. I really wanted to hire him, but I couldn't. What would I do with him? He could never file a report for me, never interface with the SEC.

Looking back on this event later, however, I wondered, *What if I had been a better friend and Randy had felt more comfortable calling me? Could I have helped him in his time of need? A time when he was alone, pressured to do what he knew he shouldn't.* We all make mistakes, but some turn out to have dire consequences.

This is where I could serve, I realized, helping people sort out the moral struggles they came across in the marketplace. A place where people were confronted every day with temptation, need, and ambition.

What would have happened if Randy and Gerard had defied their boss? They might have gotten fired; they almost surely would have suffered, but in time, these two decent, honorable people would have found work. In business, the best usually persevere, though it can involve hardship along the way.

For Randy and Gerard, they had a choice to make: go along or push back. It is easy to say push back, but what if we are living paycheck to paycheck? The decision then is much harder. We are trained to make the boss happy and provide for our families; pushing back puts this all at risk. We know what Jesus would do, but what is the secret ingredient that gave Jesus confidence to proceed? Simply put, it was faith in God. The more we practice and pursue a relationship with God through Jesus, the stronger our faith grows, girding us to confront difficult situations.

✞ ✞ ✞

In reflecting on my career and life, I realized that I had learned two very important lessons that are closely connected to the teachings of Jesus. While, regretfully, I did not always demonstrate these behaviors, I now believe they are critical aspects of thriving in today's marketplace. The first is to be wary but kind. Jesus describes this as being *"wise as serpents and innocent as doves."* (Matthew 10:16) A reminder that not all have our best interest at heart, and as Jesus told his disciples, *"I am sending you out like sheep into the midst of wolves."* (Matthew 10:16)

As our Foot Locker brand grew in stature, our senior management wondered about changing our name. Foot Locker was the dominant revenue producer of the company, which was still listed as the Woolworth Company, a remnant of its past. The obvious choice was to administratively change the name to the Foot Locker Corporation. However, when we approached a PR firm with this question, they sent us off in a different direction. They came back and recommended we change our name to an obscure one they'd come up with—the Venator Group—and then submitted a $3 million invoice. When we, the employees, were told about the new name, we were stunned. *What? Why? Are you serious?* Even our shareholders were shocked. In fact, one of our largest shareholders filed a motion to change our name to Foot Locker and not Venator. The proxy fight occurred just after I was made CFO. Great. We had a proxy fight while we were just trying to stay in business. *Why not just give in to the employees and investors and name the company what it should be named?* I asked myself. The fight was on!

The proxy fight was embarrassing. Wall Street thought it was stupid, and the Woolworth Corporation had wasted $3 million searching for a name that no one understood, Venator. Our CEO was happy with the Venator name. He barely won the proxy fight and kept the name intact. But soon after, both executives that had been fighting for the name left. And when Matt Serra was made CEO in 2001, we immediately changed our name to Foot Locker.

Soon after, I was playing golf with an executive from the accounting firm KPMG and two other men who knew of this incident and the PR firm that came up with Venator. The other men didn't know who I was, so one of them was, to say the least, not discreet.

"You wouldn't believe how Foot Locker came up with the name the Venator Group. The PR firm couldn't come up with a name that fit. Then one night at dinner a partner was expressing his frustration and his daughter asked, 'Why not call it Venator?' When asked why, she replied, 'That's what a Jedi cruiser ship is called. You know...from *Star Wars*.'"

The man from KPMG pulled him aside. "Do you know who you're playing golf with?" he asked, pointing at me. "That's Bruce Hartman, the CFO of Venator, who paid three million dollars for the name of a Jedi cruiser ship."

Great, I said to myself, *all the silliness we had to go through at a cost of $3 million was so that a PR firm could earn a fee and not care about what was right for our company.*

The four of us didn't talk much on the way home. The night had grown cold.

✝ ✝ ✝

The second lesson I was taught early in my career, and in turn taught future employees, was to focus on what counts. Jesus would say to his disciples, ***"If anyone will not welcome you or listen to your words, shake off the dust from your feet as you leave that house or town."*** (Matthew 10:14) In other words stay focused on your mission and don't get distracted by those who won't help. Certainly, Jesus knew that many times there were distractions caused by self-interest and the personal agendas of others that could move the disciples off course. He implored them to stay focused on the goal of revealing God's values.

In a business the most important goal to stay focused on is generating enough cash to pay your employees, pay your bills, and return profits to the investors. Activities that threaten this basic tenet of business are to be avoided. The old saying "cash is king" applies here, the primary goal and lifeblood of every commercial enterprise.

When I came to Foot Locker as a controller, I quickly noticed that the cash flow was out of balance; we were spending too much on items that wouldn't generate cash, such as consultants, large capital programs that served to only create better résumés for those doing the projects, and cute systems that helped some employees win the favor of their vendors. The CFO was very frustrated with the amount of money being spent and had little political capital to be listened to. The then CEO, Roger Farah, counted on the treasurer to complete the annual cash forecast. The then treasurer was frustrated, because he also couldn't make the cuts required to balance our cash. The treasurer's name was John Cannon, and he called me at the company's financial offices at Camp Hill to tell me that he and his assistant, Peter Brown, were coming to see me.

Camp Hill, across the river from Harrisburg, Pennsylvania, is not a tourist location. It is a long drive from New York City and its biggest hotel, while comfortable, is hardly the Waldorf. The fact that they were coming to my office didn't bode well.

They were ushered into a conference room where I was already waiting. John stared at me. "You know, Bruce," he said, "they're spending a lot of money that we don't have."

Both John and Peter had already talked to the CFO, but couldn't seem to resolve the cash issue through our collective boss.

Here's my dilemma, I said to myself. *We've got tens of thousands of employees, and if we can't fix this, they're all going to lose their jobs. I've got a wonderful wife and four lovely daughters I need to support. I'm going to lose my job. They weren't listening to the warnings of their treasurer. The company will go under unless I try to help.*

It seemed to me that the only recourse was to go over the CFO's head to the board itself.

I called Marc Katz, an assistant controller and a brilliant strategist. I told him the issue and asked that he come to my house, where we shared beers and, with a mutual desire to save the company, began to carve out a plan. Just a complaint to the board wouldn't cut it. We needed a proposal, even if it was more a Trojan horse than an airtight plan. We needed to get the board's attention and get them focused on our company's desperate situation.

We came up with the concept of Corporate Shared Services, under which all the supplies, utilities, and other expenses would be bought by one person in each division, with all the paperwork consolidated into one office, and all shipping and handling controlled by one executive, me. I would give up my job as corporate controller and become the head of this new division, which would mean losing my title as public officer, limiting my effectiveness, but I didn't care. What counted was that we needed to help save our company. I knew someone on the board would ask me, "Why are you doing this?"

I was sure they thought of me highly; I had been honest in the past, and several of the board members had become strong advisors to me. I knew they would listen. One of the board members, Chris Sinclair, was the most direct. "You know you'd be losing your officer title," he said. "Why would you do that?"

"Because I've got to do something to help save the company," I told him. "It doesn't matter what happens to me. We are running out of money."

I realize this sounds disingenuous, but I meant it without reservation. The board approved Corporate Shared Services (coincidently many companies have since adopted the same process), and we saved twenty to thirty million dollars. More important, we alerted and focused the board towards our precarious financial situation and they started selling buildings, like the famous New York City landmark the Woolworth Building. Woolworth Germany got sold. Still, we almost ran out of cash. In February 1999, the stock fell to three dollars a share. We were more than a billion dollars in debt and I was made CFO of Woolworth/Foot Locker, a public officer once more. And we began our slow climb back, able to focus on what counted. This riveted focus saved our company.

Later, an article in *Fortune* magazine praised us for saving Foot Locker. I didn't do it alone. It took my first CEO, Roger Farah; it took Lauren Peters, it took Mark Katz, Peter Brown, John Cannon, and Matt Serra, the future CEO. It took an open-minded board. It took a group of people who stayed focused on what counts.

Many lessons were learned in that journey. The most important was learned later: Jesus and my neighbor are more important than myself.

And if you read this chapter as a parable about honesty, transparency, teamwork, and faith—it took Jesus to get there.

CHAPTER 3

JESUS, THE MARKETPLACE EXPERT

"One does not live by bread alone, but by every word that comes from the mouth of God."

−MATTHEW 4:4

Jesus was around thirty when he was baptized and then spent forty days in the wilderness, where he faced and overcame trials and temptation. Jesus was then free to begin his mission to reveal God's values to humankind, and specifically morality and ethics for the first-century marketplace.

- How to thrive and be ethical at the same time.
- How to treat others.
- How to recognize that the source of all good comes from God.
- How to have a personal relationship with God.

In essence, Jesus's moral emphasis was on "self-worth, not net worth," and it was a message he preached in the Judean and Galilean markets. These were the places where daily life happened. People worked and struggled to earn a living. They bartered, sold their goods, created artifacts from shoes to ceramics, made money or lost it. They were prey to con men and cheats, and as in markets today, they were often exploited by men cleverer and more unscrupulous than they. They battled throughout their lives to rise above the temptation to get back at the offenders and avoid falling into the traps of greed and fear. When they had turned in the past to their religious leaders for help, they had been provided with legalistic answers—no help at all.

Jesus came among them to reveal a different way, a way embraced by God. He came to show them the moral path that kept them connected to God. Jesus came to show them that serving God and being successful could both be part of a connected life. To show them that temptation and the lure of money and power were the distractions to this path.

What is not widely discussed is that prior to his baptism and experience in the wilderness, Jesus had spent most of his life as a marketplace worker, a carpenter, a craftsman, a skilled artisan. We know from the earliest version of the Gospels that his profession was *tekton*, an honorific term for "artisan," usually associated with a carpenter, builder, or woodworker. He would have attained this level by initially learning his craft from his father, as was the custom in the first century, and then becoming more involved with other tradespeople. Over time, he would have progressed as a woodworker to the level of *tekton*, now able to help support his family and pay his bills.

Into this commercial world Jesus went to teach people to do good. To do good—not to gain something of material value, but to *be* something of value.

Jesus built an authenticity in the marketplace, where he had bartered, engaged in contract negotiations, and sold his wares. He walked amid the smells of fresh-baked bread and spices—and the treachery, double-dealing, and cheating that too often prevailed in his work environment. Probably he was also exploited by the money changers and endured abusive pricing practices, as did all his honest colleagues.

But he was different: He was the incarnation of God, sent into the world to preach God's revelations and God's purpose for humankind. He was sent into the world as a redeemer, and the embodiment of God's will.

After his work life was completed, Jesus was baptized by John the Baptist. As Jesus rose up out of the water, God spoke: *"This is my Son, the Beloved, with whom I am well pleased."* (Matthew 3:17) Underlying these words are the identification of who Jesus was: God himself in human form preparing to begin God's mission.

In the Bible, when we see capitalized letters in the middle of a sentence, it is a direct identification of God. Here, we notice the words "Son" and "Beloved" are capitalized. Jesus is sanctified by being identified as God.

There was one final step. Jesus still had to undergo his time in the wilderness, a vast and dark place with no friends, no relatives, no resources. A place of abject desolation. For forty days, Jesus fasted. For forty days he was alone in this barren spot. At the end he was famished, both physically and spiritually. He was alone and hungry, ripe for temptation by Satan.

Jesus was given the chance to turn stones into bread, a temptation to solve his hunger. Tortured and tormented, all he had to do was give in to natural human needs. Give in, and Satan, the dark prince of evil, would resolve his misery. But Jesus resisted temptation and natural human tendencies by saying, ***"One does not live by bread alone, but by every word that comes from the mouth of God."*** (Matthew 4:4).

A second test followed. He was asked by Satan to throw himself down from the top of a pinnacle to see if God would save him, and in this way prove God's existence. When we ourselves have had to endure a difficult crisis in our lives—our own personal wilderness, where we feel alone and desperate—we have cried out in lamentation to test God's existence in our lives: "Does God exist?"

In this spot, Jesus demonstrates and models the faith of God's existence and says, *"Do not put the Lord your God to the test."* (Matthew 4:7)

Finally, Satan offers to give Jesus power over all the kingdoms of the world in exchange for leaving his relationship with God. Once more, Jesus was steadfast. *"Away with you, Satan! for it is written, 'Worship the Lord your God and serve only Him.'"* (Matthew 4:10)

Here was an extraordinary example of modeling and will. Jesus remained true to his mission. He threw off the temptations that would have eased his physical discomfort, because giving in would have created a lesser existence, an existence without God.

How many of us in the marketplace have experienced our own wilderness, alone in a desolate place? I certainly have, as have most of my friends. If we haven't experienced this wilderness, we are long overdue. In this place we look for sustenance but find none. We feel incorrectly that God and our colleagues have abandoned us. We seek ways to escape. We lose our focus on what counts. We become desperate and our faith is tested. We fortunate ones find help in Jesus. Jesus models for us when we remember Jesus's own time in the wilderness. Jesus remained riveted to the only way out: He remained true to God.

Henry Parsons Crowell found himself through Jesus. His father died at age thirty-six of tuberculosis. He himself nearly died from the same disease. Because of his father's death, Henry had to work to earn the money to keep his family afloat, and was unable to get a high school diploma. He lost his first wife and was left to parent their child alone. In spite of many years of personal setbacks, he continued to remain a faithful Christian and to pursue a business life. And as time wore on, he began to have some success in business, enough to buy the Quaker Mill in Ravenna, Ohio, in 1881 and turn it into a company called Quaker Oats. There he made one small change: Instead of selling his cereal in large barrels, as was the custom, he introduced the small containers we're familiar with today, allowing him to sell his product directly to the customer. Soon Quaker Oats became available in grocery stores throughout the country and his company grew to become one of America's largest corporations. During the depression of 1893, Quaker Oats became an affordable staple for thousands of American families.

As his company became self-sufficient, Henry and his new wife, Susan, traveled the country, working for God through service and encouraging other tycoons in the business world to rethink their values, including John D. Rockefeller. Today, we see similar behavior in people like Bill and Melinda Gates, who created an organization designed to help the world with a large portion of their wealth. In some years, Henry and his wife would donate to as many as 100 charitable organizations. He worked for the Lord. "If my life can be lived so as to please him in every way," he said, "I'll be supremely happy."

Crowell died in 1944 on a commuter train with a Bible in his hand, leaving a large trust, with this directive to the trustees: "To carry out Mr. Crowell's wishes to honor the Lord who he loved and served during his life on earth."

The trustees have kept his wish alive. Each year they issue close to 150 grants in various fields, totaling millions of dollars, proving that well past his death Crowell is still working for God. "The Cereal Tycoon," as he was called, created a life of riches for himself simply by changing the way Quaker Oats were sold and remaining steadfastly committed to his life with Jesus. A life that began with enormous hurdles and ended with spectacular success. Henry Crowell was inspired by Jesus. Because he worked tirelessly for "the Lord he loved."

† † †

When Jesus passed the tests in the wilderness, he was ready to start his mission, and headed off to the world and to the marketplace. But first he had to assemble a team—not just any team, but one that in effect represented the people of his world. Andrew, Peter, James, and John were fishermen; Matthew was a tax collector; Jesus was a carpenter. They were everyday people from everyday life. They had to work to pay their bills.

Their mission was simple: to serve God. None were from the religious elite or from the aristocracy. Those men were Jesus's main antagonists. They had created a power structure that was opposed to the values of God. Jesus was offering business solutions counter to that. They had imposed rules to support their base. Over time they corrupted the original Ten Commandments of God by adding human strictures. They argued that what they were doing was called tradition, but they bent the message of God. While they interpreted God's Commandments legalistically, even their legalism was flawed. Importantly, their rules avoided the *spirit* of the Commandments. Jesus and his band of twelve disciples were in Judea to change this world, to change the future, to help the common person work and survive in the marketplace, living by the *spirit* of God's laws.

Jesus used simple language; he didn't engage in long, flowery discourse. He spoke in plain language that helped create a greater understanding among those he came to serve and help. His words themselves are part of his glory. He taught through parables that were principally directed to the marketplace, stories that illustrated the original intent of God's purpose. Thomas Rausch, the author of *Who Is Jesus?*, described the parables by saying: "They challenge our customary way of seeing the world, draw us out of complacency, force us to ask questions, to rethink our values." They affect us even today at our core. Imagine the effect they had on first-century society and its marketplace!

Jesus selected his apostles as if they were human parables. Because they had little vested interest in the prevailing power structure and traditions of the religious elite or aristocracy, they could move beyond the entanglements of the prevailing flawed system. Having the right culture in place was paramount to the mission and these were the people who would form this culture. Honest people who looked for possibilities and were not chained to tradition.

Jesus and his team ventured into the real world—a world of people which required the average person to work in order to survive, a world in search of meaning, a world confused by a corrupt power system, a world often filled with treachery and deceit. A world Jesus knew well as a former member of it and as God. He had developed an authenticity by working among the average workers; he had become identifiable to them.

The marketplace of Judea consisted of potters, basket makers, tailors, carpenters, bakers, wine vendors, jewelers—tradesmen supplying simple goods for a generally poor population. The streets were redolent of herbs and spices, or freshly made candy, freshly baked bread. Craftsmen hammered metal to make jewelry, and the sounds reverberated through the streets. All hawked their wares in a chorus of salesmanship; even so long ago, advertisements festooned pillars and walls.

The rich would buy at the Xystus Market in the wealthy sections of Jerusalem, a place similar to today on Fifth Avenue or Michigan Avenue or Rodeo Drive. In smaller cities and towns commerce took place on dirt paths, or if communities were wealthy, the streets were made of well-sculpted stone. "Buy low and sell high" was the philosophy of all, as it is today. Throughout there were money changers, like today's hedge fund managers, and a particularly nasty group called tax collectors who preyed on the weak to fulfill quotas for their Roman masters.

People in the marketplace, good and bad, struggled with morality. Do I point out the knot in the wood if the potential buyer doesn't see it? Do I allow slow payments to establish a long-term relationship with my client, or insist on the money today? Much as in the modern world, temptation existed in every show, every deal, every transaction.

Into this world arrived Jesus, to show merchants and buyers God's way. He didn't theorize or preach to make his points. He talked in terms the marketplace could understand, in their language, and in parables they could easily understand. In Matthew 9:16, Jesus says, ***"No one sews a piece of unshrunk cloth on an old cloak, for the patch pulls away from the cloak, and a worse tear is made."***

Common sense, in fact and in language. Clothes and garments had to last a long time in Judea. Repairing them could be done haphazardly—unshrunk cloth on an old cloak—or, if you wanted the repair to last, the right way—shrunk cloth made specifically to cover the hole. There are many meanings to this parable, but overall it is simply a suggestion of prudence in what we do—and that what we do should be done with quality. A simple message the marketplace worker would understand: prudence and morality.

Mike Zawosky was a pain in the butt. "Is the project finished yet?" I'd ask. "You'll have it by this afternoon," he'd reply. "I have a few more things to check." And, on time or not, he'd produce it. He did things his way, and the final product was invariably impeccable, but usually late. Mike couldn't be rushed.

With each new project I asked him to undertake, or report I needed him to write, the result was far better than anything I could produce myself, but it meant going through the same dance. "I'm in a hurry," I'd snap at him. He'd smile. "Boss, not yet." Infuriating!

When I first arrived at Foot Locker, I quickly realized that Mike was one of the people I could trust. He was buried in some department that produced nothing but had a fancy title: the Process Replanning Department. One day I asked him what his department did. "Plan, design processes, and hold meetings," he answered. "What gets implemented?" I asked. He grinned. "Nothing. That's somebody else's job."

Mike's boss had set up his department to produce theory; no results were expected, and in turn there was no accountability. Good for Mike's boss's résumé, useless for Foot Locker. This led to one of my easiest early decisions: disband the department and persuade Mike to work directly for me.

I promoted Mike a number of times over the next ten years; his responsibilities grew. And each time he'd work at his own pace, each time the project was fulfilled without blemish. Each project was completed thoughtfully and with the right code of business ethics. Despite my badgering, he would never put unshrunk cloth on an old cloak.

Today Mike is CEO of a Midwestern retailer. You won't be surprised when I tell you it's thriving. Yet I'm sure some of its board members get frustrated because nothing gets done until it's done correctly.

Jesus's dinner guests were often the previously mentioned sinners of the local business world. At this table, he tried to change values. His message centered on self-worth—not net worth—and many, including those notorious thugs of the Judean marketplace, the tax collectors, listened. Matthew, who became one of Jesus's apostles, was a tax collector.

Other than shepherds, tax collectors appear the most of any profession in the Gospels. Some modern day English scholars criticize them for this, saying tax collectors are overused in the stories of the Gospels. But Jesus and the Gospel writers were making a critical point with this repetition. By selecting the most disliked and potentially dangerous of all in the first-century marketplace, Jesus was emphasizing that even the lowest on the morality scale were available for redemption—a point Jesus was hammering home not to produce great literature, but to reassure his listeners that all could be saved.

Taxes were remitted to the local ruling Roman officials, and the punishment for the tax collector who did not provide Rome with its quota could be harsh, even including death. The collectors were tough; they had to be, or else. Their goal was to collect their quota, but since they had to earn a living, they generally collected more than Rome's share, sometimes with force, sometimes with guile. Often, a tax collector would approach a local merchant randomly and demand excess taxes for a trumped-up reason. The rules were vague and indiscriminate, and the burden on the collectors was heavy, but many became wealthy off their excess collections. Since they were largely recruited from the local population, it's no wonder they were hated and feared by their community.

Jesus knew them well; he had probably encountered some of them during his time as an artisan.

At one time in his three-year mission, Jesus traveled through Jericho, a city at the bottom of a steep climb to Jerusalem. Here he met with Zacchaeus, a wealthy tax collector who had heard of Jesus and was so anxious to see him that he climbed a large tree to watch Jesus approach. Jesus stopped at the base of the tree. ***"Zacchaeus, hurry and come down; for I must stay at your house today."*** (Luke 19:5) Zacchaeus was astounded that Jesus knew who he was, cared about him, and wanted to visit. Overwhelmed with emotion that God was speaking to him through his Son, he declared, "I will give half of my possessions to the poor and those I have defrauded. I will pay four times the amount." Jesus, recognizing this change and repentance, promised him salvation. ***"For the Son of Man came to seek out and save the lost."*** (Luke 19:10)

Yearly visits from IRS tax collectors occurred in all the companies I worked at. Generally, they were despised and mistrusted, relegated to some back office or even the cellar, to do their accounting work. Early in my career, I was advised by a wise employee, Jack Litter, to be nice to them. "They have a tough job and will appreciate your treating them as equals," he told me. I carried this advice to every job I took, and my dealings with the IRS were always fair and without hostility. "Treat them with respect and they will treat you with respect," Jack said. Jesus would have recommended the same approach.

At Foot Locker, our auditor from KPMG recommended we hire a man named Bob McHugh. He was trustworthy, positive, and competent, the auditor reported. We hired McHugh as our vice president of taxes, and he could not have been more helpful. Bob agreed with my approach to the IRS collectors and extended it: He gave them an office on the main floor of our corporate headquarters, allowed them access to all our financial dealings, and insisted on total transparency. "Why not, when we have nothing to hide?" Bob said when asked about his strategy.

After a few years, the IRS asked us to try something new: real-time auditing, a pilot program they wanted to institute to speed up the post-audit process. Because of our good relations with them, we were chosen to be the first American company to try their new method.

The program was a success. The IRS had up-to-date information, and our audits were finished when we closed the books. The value to Foot Locker was the elimination of the risk of future audits. The value to the IRS was a clearer picture of our tax liabilities: We didn't pay any more—or less—than we owed. Partnership, as Bob knew it would, turned out to be more effective than antagonism and suspicion. After all, yesterday's and today's tax collectors are human and number among God's people.

✝ ✝ ✝

Jesus is often believed to have said that earning a decent living is wrong. What he actually meant was that the covetous pursuit of money is wrong. He wasn't against earning a living; Jesus was against earning a living by defrauding our neighbors and moving away from having a relationship with God. Jesus knew that families and individuals needed money, and that they had to work for it. In fact, as an artisan, historians suggest that Jesus probably earned a wage comparable to others of his day. Jesus knew and knows we all have to pay our bills.

Jesus was also a friend of the wealthy. Two rich benefactors, Nicodemus and Joseph of Arimathea, not only provided him with support, but were responsible for his tomb, and the perfumes and shroud needed for the burial. Jesus wasn't biased against any social group, he was biased *toward* those who lived for God, who loved God and their neighbor. Both Nicodemus, who, interestingly, was a Pharisee, and Joseph had engaged with Jesus in seeking the truth. Both men learned that truth. Both men, who were from the elite, showed that even though they were part of the structure Jesus was trying to change, they were people who pursued God and wanted a different life.

Jesus knew the value of hard work. He was more concerned with citizens who did not have a giving nature, who protected their assets when others were in need. He was interested in a person's self-worth, not net worth. Jesus loved a generous heart.

At one point, he was approached by a rich businessman who believed Jesus was the Messiah and told him he wanted eternal life. He'd lived well, loved his neighbor, followed all the Commandments. But Jesus exposed the flaw in the man's heart by stating, *"If you wish to be perfect, go, sell all your possessions and give the money to the poor, and you will have treasure in heaven; then come, follow me."* (Matthew 19:21)

The man couldn't comply, for he had many possessions—indeed, he was possessed by his possessions. He lacked a generous heart. Jesus had tested the man. The man had earned his money and his possessions honestly, but his heart was trapped by them. He approached being good as a way to gain eternal life. He was looking for a quid pro quo. He didn't approach being good as something of value in itself.

"Again I tell you," Jesus said, *"it is easier for a camel to go through the eye of a needle than for someone who is rich to enter the kingdom of God."* (Matthew 19:24) One theory holds that "the eye of the needle" refers specifically to a small gate at the entrance to Jerusalem. No camel could go through it unless it knelt, a symbol of humility.

It is less about wealth, Jesus believed, than about avoiding the lure of it. With money, Jesus preached, comes the responsibility of humility and charity, a recognition that our hearts should shy away from being possessed by wealth and turn to helping others.

Jesus knew the lure and temptations that existed in the first-century marketplace, and warned that money and possessions can and will warp our hearts. Wealth can turn our heads from our neighbors in need and from God.

✝ ✝ ✝

When Matt Serra took over as CEO of Foot Locker, he and Tim Finn, the president of the U.S. Foot Locker division, helped create the annual "Sneaker Ball," the best way, we felt, to fund the Foot Locker

Foundation, established to help disadvantaged youth. Employees, vendors, friends, and sports celebrities attended the affair, dressed in formal wear but wearing their favorite sneakers. Millions of dollars were raised each year.

When Tim approached Matt with his idea of a ball, Matt's response was immediate: "Of course." Tim's mission was to give the money raised to urban youth, making it possible for them to go to college or simply to have a better future. Tim was an extraordinarily good businessman and he showed the generous heart that Jesus desired.

This was a remarkable step for a company that had just waged a two-year battle for survival. Tim recognized our need to give back to the community that helped Foot Locker survive, generosity that both recognized a community in need and made a statement to our employees about sharing.

In the marketplace where Jesus walked, two factions of the religious elite stood in constant conflict: the Pharisees and the Sadducees. The Sadducees consisted of the wealthy, the chief priests, and the high priest. They held the majority of the seventy seats on the ruling assembly, the Sanhedrin, roughly equivalent to our senate. If the Sanhedrin was compliant to Rome, they were allowed to set the rules by which marketplace workers had to live. However, they misinterpreted the words of the Bible to support their power and, in Jesus's time, denied the existence of the spiritual world, a compromise made to gain personal power that ignored the words of God.

The Pharisees were mostly middle class. They championed legalistic views of the words of God. They, too, purposely misinterpreted the Bible—*look how religious we are*, they proclaimed. They made sure everyone saw them pray. They conspicuously donated money to charity. It wasn't God's approval they sought, but the approval of their peers. Over time, thanks to their shrewd marketing, their traditions became as important or more important than those recommended by the Bible. Even though they represented a small portion of the marketplace, they announced their way as the only way and expected the marketplace to follow.

The Sadducees and Pharisees banded together to discredit Jesus and his teachings for life and the marketplace. Jesus knew their opposition was more about maintaining their own power than expanding on God's values.

In one of Jesus's parables, a Pharisee prays, "I thank you that I am not like other people: thieves, rogues, adulterers or even like this tax collector. I fast twice a week; I give a tenth of all my income." (Luke 18:11–12)

A tax collector stood far off. He, too, prayed, though he was too ashamed to look up to heaven. "God, be merciful to me, a sinner!" he said imploringly. The tax collector had heard what his critics said, and had succumbed to their beliefs. But Jesus, without the lens of unsympathetic judgment, saw a human being, one not to be despised but in need of assistance. ***I tell you, this man went down to his home justified rather than the other; for all who exalt themselves will be humbled, but all who humble themselves will be exalted.*** (Luke 18:14)

The religious elite had bent the purpose of God. They were no better than—and not much different from—the average worker, but they surrounded themselves with legalisms to justify their positions and to sanctify their lives. They ignored the grace of God given to them freely through Jesus.

When I started at Foot Locker, it was hard to navigate the excessive rules and traditions that were sinking the company. People couldn't make progress; they were tied up by the bureaucratic regulations created by their bosses. Hidden away unspectacularly among Foot Locker workers was a man named Joe Bongiorno. He knew everyone and all the rules, and knew how to work around the bureaucracy. Joe was a castoff, working for someone who didn't realize he could get anything done. He was tucked away where the pretty, powerful people couldn't see him—a sled dog, not a poodle. But when I needed help, Joe was there; when I wanted a special project done, Joe completed it on time. When the time for his evaluation came, however, his managers wanted to give him an average review. They entirely missed his specialness. Joe was plainspoken; he hadn't gone to a great university like Stanford. He was humble, self-effacing, and invaluable. He was a fit in the new culture of change.

Joe was present at every critical juncture of our recovery, largely unnoticed but always standing on the wall, defending Foot Locker, the company he had worked for during his entire career. When we had an opening for vice president of supply chain, we promoted Joe. Many of the elite scoffed at his rise—he wasn't smooth enough. He didn't use the latest lingo or flowery words. But Joe reorganized our supply system, allowing us to get products into our stores within three days. Our vendors loved him. He got right to the point and fixed their complaints. Our stores appreciated Joe's ability to listen and learn. He always worked better than budget. He made our company hum.

Buried in every company is a Joe or Juliet who is one of the cornerstones. They work without glory, but get things done. They are the sled dogs of corporations. They know how to avoid the "Pharisees of overregulation."

One day, Joe saw me make the sign of the cross and took me aside. "Try it this way," he said, and added a gesture of thankfulness, a pressing of the mouth to thank God for our blessings. I'm not sure my pastor would agree, but I took it as a symbol of humility.

Joe wanted to know God. He was, as many are, tongue-tied in his ability to express his faith. But those of us who knew him well found in him a deep-rooted commitment to God and, through Jesus, to his coworkers and neighbors.

He retired from Foot Locker, proud that he and his team had built a great supply chain. As he preferred, he left without much fanfare. He just "did his job," he told me.

Jesus likes sled dogs.

✝ ✝ ✝

My wife has a practical view of the marketplace. She has three principles that apply to its people:

- We have to pay our bills.
- We have to work to pay our bills.
- We want a purpose and a connection with God.

These are simple truths for the 160 million people who work in our marketplace today, a place where most of us will work for most of our lives. It was always so. The need to pay the bills prevailed in the Judean marketplace as well. So did the need to have a purpose and a connection with God.

Jesus knew this of course. It is the reality of human life. He first went to the marketplace to work as an artisan, which allowed him to develop an authenticity. Second, he passed the test of temptation. And finally, he devoted much of his mission on earth to helping working people by using parables spoken in the language of the marketplace. He avoided overly complex theories and got to the point.

In the Gospel of Matthew, there's a section called "The Three Parables." They show the sensitivity that Jesus used to bridge between God and the marketplace world. He said:

"The Kingdom of heaven is like treasure hidden in a field, which someone found and hid; then in his joy he goes and sells all he has and buys that field." (Matthew 13:44)

"Again, the kingdom of heaven is like a merchant in search of fine pearls; on finding one pearl of great value, he went and sold all he had and bought it." (Matthew 13:45–46)

"Again, the kingdom of heaven is like a net that was thrown into the sea and caught fish of every kind; when it was full they drew it ashore, sat down, and put the good into the baskets but threw out the bad." (Matthew 13:47–50)

Note that these parables are intended for a specific audience—the Judean marketplace—yet have equal value for today and tomorrow. As in most of Jesus's parables, the language is simple and designed to help the worker understand.

Jesus knew his audience and his mission.

CHAPTER 4

JESUS, FAITHFUL AND ETHICAL EMPLOYEE

"Very truly, I tell you, the Son can do nothing on his own, but only what he sees the Father doing; for whatever the Father does, the Son does likewise."

–JOHN 5:19

Theologians use the word *kenosis* to define the emptying of the human self to be closer to God. When Jesus was twenty-four hours from the Crucifixion, he went to the Garden of Gethsemane and three times asked God if it was God's will that his life be taken from him. If the answer was yes, could he at least be relieved of the horrible events surrounding his death: the beatings, the humiliation, the gruesome nailing to the cross. He prayed he could separate his human desires from God's desires. Jesus prayed, ***"My Father, if it is possible, let this cup pass from me; yet not what I want but what you want."*** (Matthew 26:39)

The Crucifixion was indeed God's will; Jesus was designated by God to be the Savior, the link between God and humankind. And so he died on the cross to absolve humankind of its sins, and in so doing he was loving God and his neighbor. He was God's faithful employee.

It's difficult for us humans to imagine Jesus's thoughts. At Gethsemane he was all by himself, wrestling with which way to go. He knew full well that God had given him only one path to follow. Jesus knew his mission took deep prayer. Three times he went and knelt humbly. Three times he searched for a different path. Three times Jesus's inner human thoughts shifted from himself to God's will, and finally Jesus submitted in humble obedience to do what God had asked.

Through *kenosis*, Jesus embodied a loyal and faithful employee. In order to serve God Jesus surrendered the natural human tendency toward personal interest. There was a job to do, and by doing his job, Jesus would be connecting humanity with God. By giving up and draining himself of personal ambition for the team, he became an effective worker on behalf of God.

His obedience reveals an important value to God: humility in the face of Almighty. Jesus was sent to earth to be a proxy for humankind in resolving sin. It meant a complete surrendering of his fears and an extraordinary commitment to God's will. Jesus could have found a momentary place for escape. For a short time, he would have been able to hide from his mission. But then he would have been forced to define himself as a quitter, unreliable to God. The eventual negative effect on Jesus would have drowned his momentary peace. With the help of prayer, for the good of humankind he was able to find the right path—God's path.

✝ ✝ ✝

In Super Bowl XLIX, on February 1, 2015, with only a few seconds left in the game, the Seattle Seahawks were poised to score on the New England Patriots and win the game. The Seahawks were on the one-yard line with three chances to push the ball across the goal line and win the Super Bowl. A yard away from victory. Then it happened! Malcolm Butler, an unheralded cornerback for the Patriots, intercepted a short pass and, with his arms held tightly around the ball, fell to the ground with a cry of triumph, assuring a Patriot victory. Miraculous? Reporters called it the greatest play ever in a Super Bowl. Actually, it was a man just doing his job.

Four years earlier, Butler had been working at a Popeyes, making $7.50 an hour. His dream was to play professional football, but he hadn't even made his community college team. He had become distracted from his dreams and his faith. He no longer was the star and he needed a new direction. He knew he had to recommit himself to football and his faith. He had his own *kenosis* moment.

He enrolled at the University of West Alabama and was named to the First-Team All-Gulf South Conference. Yet at the NFL draft combine, his forty-yard dash was so slow he went undrafted. More recommitment. Back home he worked on his speed and eventually was invited to the Patriots training camp.

There he was always prepared; his teammates called him "Scrappy." He played every drill, every snap, as though the game itself were at stake. But he didn't make the starting team and for most of the season sat on the bench. Slowly, though, he got more playing time, and thus he was on the field for the "miraculous" interception. The motto for the players and coaching staff in the 2014 season was "Do your job." Malcolm committed himself to this motto and through the season continued to garner more playing time.

Prior to the famous play, the coaches on the sidelines noticed confusion and an unusual formation by the Seattle Seahawks. The Patriots wanted a new formation that included having Malcolm on the field. But Malcolm was on the sidelines. The coaches yelled to Malcolm, "Go, get on the field." Instead of calling time-out to preserve a few seconds, coach Bill Belichick, who had noticed this glimmer of confusion on the Seattle sidelines, said, "I got this."

There Malcolm was on the field, with thirty seconds to go and the Seahawks poised to score. He had seen the Seahawk formation before on film. Ernie Adams, the video scout, had seen it, too, and had shown it to the coaching staff in practice that week to help prepare the players, including Malcom. His partner cornerback, Brandon Browner, also knew what was coming. Browner whispered to Butler, "They are going to throw at you and try to pick you before you get there. I will shield you."

The ball was snapped and it worked out just the way the Patriots had prepared. It appeared like a miracle, but it was actually a group of people doing their job. The motto for the players worked.

After the game, a major step in Malcom Butler's long climb was over. He told the reporters that he was blessed and thanked God. Malcom has gone on to become one of the best cornerbacks in the NFL. In February 2017, filmmakers announced they were making a movie of his life.

Jesus was also an honest employee—for God. He would remind those around him that his power came from God and would only act in a manner that supported his message from God. His words that I quote at the beginning of the chapter were spoken early in his journey for God. He knew his mission. As did Malcolm Butler.

Eighteen years ago, a young man, recommended by a friend, walked into my office at Foot Locker seeking a job. His name was Kevin Darrington. Quickly I recognized what my friend, Mike Powell, had seen in Kevin. He was positive, highly ethical, and knew how to listen and learn. He didn't have a résumé filled with awards and accolades, nor did he come from a prestigious college. He was just very sincere, knew how to get things done, and always knew his job.

He became the youngest of our core group that helped save Foot Locker from bankruptcy. He was our "Tigger," committed and enthusiastic, equal in smarts and dedication, if not in age. Over the years I watched him grow and promoted him when openings occurred. He left to become CFO of a company in Buffalo, Tops Markets, where he also thrived. He died suddenly in September 2016, leaving a widow and five children.

He would always call me "sir" and women "ma'am," and his style was easy to work with. I would give him a goal and ask his opinion, and his responses were invariably carefully considered. When he disagreed with anyone, he disagreed politely, and because of his good manners and intelligence he was listened to and respected. Others were happy to help him in areas where he was weak. He focused on completing his tasks and shunned the politics that arise in every major project.

He always remained committed to doing his job as assigned. At our weekly updates, he had thought through his "to do" list and anticipated what was next. When asked to do something outside his area of responsibility, he did it without complaint. He stood there next to us in saving our company. When thanked, he always replied, "Just doing my job, boss."

His sister gave his eulogy and described his personal life, showing those of us inhabiting his work world that his strengths carried over to his family and friends. He was a faithful Christian with a simple theology: love God and love your neighbor. It wasn't a sophisticated philosophy, but always wanting to be good, he lived by it. At work or at home, he embodied the spirit of *kenosis* and stayed riveted on completing his tasks. Kevin always did his job.

After the eulogy, a friend summed up: "A life well lived." Another described Kevin as "a beautiful soul." He was indeed: a beautiful soul and a faithful employee.

✝ ✝ ✝

When we visit The Parable of the Talents (Matthew 25:14–30), we see another story heavily directed to the marketplace, and we see Jesus's views of what is most desirable to an employer in an employee. He tells the tale of a business owner embarking on a long journey, who gives three employees coins to be put to work improving the business while he is gone.

The first employee, his boss's favorite, receives five coins, which he doubles. The second, not as favored as the first, receives two coins and creates two more. The third and least trustworthy employee gets one coin, which he promptly buries in a hole.

When the boss returns, he meets with each employee to check on his progress. The first now has ten coins. "Well done, good and trustworthy employee," the boss says. "I will put you in charge of many things; enter into the joy of your employer."

The second now has four coins, twice what he started with. The employer praises him as well and says that he, too, has earned the "joy of your employer."

The third employee makes excuses for not doing better. When criticized, he blames the employer for being harsh. The employee is fired.

The parable reveals something central to Jesus's mission: the importance of not only just doing our job, but also extending our job by adding value. For those of us wishing to "enter into the joy of our employers," this extension of our job is critical. Do your job well in order to add value to it.

The parable applies to our faith lives as well. God gives us tasks, both at work and in life, and gives us the gift of talents (an ancient word for coins) to accomplish them. Jesus's message speaks to how we handle the talents we are given. The more we help others, the more we will be given to help. Our faithfulness toward God will expand our mission and in turn create a greater sense of self-worth.

The parable is written in words that the first-century Judean worker could understand. There are no subtleties, there is no extensive doctrine. There are no multisyllabic words written in a scholastic manner. The words are as easy to understand now as they were then, and they apply in the same way.

Jesus's parables hold many meanings and connections. Here, we connect our role in our work to the task of serving God. Perform well at work, Jesus is saying, and also as faithful believers.

On Sunday evenings, I would prepare for the next week by writing down in a little black book everything the other employees and I had to do. Some weeks the tasks numbered over one hundred individual "to dos." Each week I visited with every employee to review his or her immediate tasks and long-term goals. Whenever possible, I would try to meet in person, avoiding dictatorial phone calls or emails.

When we talked face-to-face, I could catch the nuances revealed by body language, by voice, by facial expression. So I did "walk-arounds," where I would drop in on people, even on those who needed little attention, even if a new task was not required.

On these walk-arounds, I always enjoyed visiting Dave Diaz, an internal auditor, a man buried deep in our organization. He kept his head down, worked hard, and paid attention to what was going on. His coworkers trusted him. He was polite, frank, and insightful.

On one of my walk-arounds, I asked Dave about a new accounting program we were installing. I hadn't been happy with the way it was performing, and I asked Dave if he could help.

After a few days, he reported back: He'd noticed a disconnect in some of the files that were feeding our new system, and told me he'd pointed them out to the computer staff and the accountants who were installing the program. Because of his warmly assertive personal communication style, instead of begrudging him, they were grateful and fixed the flaw. Things went smoothly from there on.

This was a simple task, handled without drama or excuses, completed without fanfare and with no request for reward. "Just doing my job," Dave said, and went on to his next mission. Years later, I got a message from Dave through LinkedIn, thanking me for the lessons I had taught him at Foot Locker. Like many others I had counseled, he gave me more credit than I deserved. Cooperative and faithful people like Dave and others got things done. I just walked around.

Dave is in his fifties now. He recently moved to Denver, where, because of his age, he had to accept a job significantly below his ability. When asked how he was able to adjust, he replied, "I do my job and what they ask me to do." Simple—and so like Dave. He has, I'm sure, entered into the "joy of his employer."

✝ ✝ ✝

One of the difficult parts of the Bible to interpret is Jesus's reference to "slaves." The word had many different meanings in the first century, and understanding some of these meanings helps us further connect the four Gospels to the first-century marketplace. Jesus and the Gospel writers didn't always use the word as we do in the 21st century—in some cases Jesus was simply referring to employees of a commercial enterprise. Today slavery is considered a horrendous practice, an oppressive hardship placed on an innocent individual, the practice itself inseparable from racism and violence. In Jesus's time, the terms "slaves" or "servants" (the word some English Bibles use) might refer to doctors, nurses, cooks, private tutors, engineers, accountants, carpenters (yes, Jesus was a "slave"), or day laborers. Slaves could earn wages and, as opposed to the slaves in America, could be indigenous.

Much of first-century society was segmented. There were rulers, masters, common people, servants, and slaves. Today, there are safeguards for workers ensuring they won't be exploited. Human rights is an accepted, valued philosophy. Then, the marketplace conformed to existing social traditions. When we see the word "slave" in the Bible, we can at times accurately substitute the word "employee."

With this knowledge we can consider another parable, "The Faithful or the Unfaithful Slave" (Matthew 24:45–51) In this story, Jesus asks us to consider our behavior when the boss isn't looking. A master goes on a journey and appoints a trusted employee to look after his estate while he is gone. The new overseer treats the other employees well; when the master returns, all is smooth and the employees are happily at work. ***Truly I tell you, he will put that one in charge of all his possessions,*** Jesus tells us. (Matthew 24:47) Conversely, he describes another overseer who mistreats subordinates when his boss is away, leaving frequently to drink at a bar rather than tend to the estate. The master returns unexpectedly and finds the estate in disarray. The employee is promptly fired.

As managers and as employees we have a responsibility to be wise and fair. If we're not, we risk our livelihood. In the "Faithful and Unfaithful Slave" parable, Jesus, using the language of the first century, is helping us not only with our behavior at work, but with our overall attitude toward life and God. We can see from this parable that a subtle change in the definition of one word, using the discipline of historical context, changes the context and further connects Jesus and the parables to the marketplace.

✟ ✟ ✟

As employees in the 21st century, we are evaluated through an annual review process. Our companies use this process to communicate to us how well we are doing and to give us our goals. Our employer is our master.

Company reviews were held in April in the businesses where I worked. As part of senior management, I was at the top of this process and attended lengthy discussions evaluating other employees. There were forms to fill out, and everything was sorted, organized, analyzed. We organized workers into five categories: superior, very good, good, needs improvement, failing.

The people who got the superior reviews always had similar characteristics: They had positive attitudes. People liked them and they liked people. They were good listeners and cared about their peers. They were trustworthy, faithful, and dedicated to getting the job done. They focused on "what counted" and were loyal both to their peers and to the company. And they were technically competent. They learned what they didn't know and held a quality-first attitude in getting their job done. These were the people who got the largest rewards. As you can see, most of their success was behavioral and cultural. It was as though they understood the parables of the talents and the faithful slave, even if they hadn't studied them.

✟ ✟ ✟

At the very beginning of Jesus's three-year mission, he gave a lengthy sermon before a large crowd, called the Sermon on the Mount, an extensive revelation of God's will to humankind. In a short thesis on the purpose of his mission (fully detailed in Matthew 5–7), he expresses radical thoughts for society and the marketplace. The sermon contains familiar ideas, such as loving your enemies, the Lord's Prayer, and the Golden Rule.

The Golden Rule as part of this Sermon reads: ***"In everything do to others as you would have them do to you; for this is the law and the prophets."*** (Matthew 7:12) This is sometimes a difficult rule to follow in the workplace. We get offended or unfairly treated, but in turn are supposed to be respectful? How do we handle ourselves in the marketplace when we've been cast aside? How do we behave well, stick to the way of God, when we've been slighted?

In my early thirties, I was promoted to divisional controller of a small division of May Department Stores. This was the first time I would manage a large group of people, and it was a major step forward in my career.

Immediately, there was a problem: Duane Bursetta, the man I was replacing, disabled and confined to a wheelchair, was from now on going to report to me. I had been told he was not capable of the job and management was pushing him aside.

Being young and new to managing large groups, I went to a friend at Human Resources and asked if the situation was as unusual as I thought. "You're right," he said. "He's disabled and the people in Corporate don't like him. They'll want you to fire him."

Great, I thought. *My first job as a senior manager is to fire a person confined to a wheelchair. How am I going to get through this?*

I met with Duane on my first day, and we talked for a long time. I discovered a person of great spiritual depth with a strong financial planning background. He was personable and friendly. I liked him.

I approached the divisional CEO, John Toler, and told him that Duane would make a good employee and that Corporate was making a mistake. "Work something out," said Toler.

I next had a candid conversation with Duane. I told him that the folks at Corporate wanted him fired, but I disagreed with them and we had to work something out that helped both him and the company. Duane acknowledged that he had been waiting for me to fire him. I then told him about my plan, that I had spoken with the divisional CEO, John, and he had agreed to let me figure a way to work this out. So, I told Duane, "You will be the head of Planning and work directly for me. If we find out that someone from Corporate is coming for a visit, you will work from home that day. Any correspondence you need to have with Corporate, put my name at the bottom." I asked Duane, "What do you think?" He replied, "I am close to fifty and disabled, this is my best option. Otherwise, I will be unemployed for a long time."

Duane and I had started a fruitful relationship. He did not resent my new prominence, and when he thought I was making a mistake he would pull me aside to give me advice. Usually, I would come to see things his way; he helped mold me into being a senior executive.

After a year, I was promoted to a larger division, Lord & Taylor in New York City, and asked if I could bring Duane with me. The divisional powers to be said yes and Duane was delighted.

"How are you going to navigate the city?" I asked him, realizing how difficult New York might be for a disabled person.

"Let me worry about that," he said.

He not only found a way to get around, everyone he worked with loved him. He was friendly, cooperative, and the best planner the company had. He never held grudges, never complained about his treatment at May Stores. He more than earned his pay, in spite of working for a company that mistreated him. He knew the Golden Rule and would not let himself react negatively toward the company that had wanted to abandon him. His standard was to treat his company the way he wanted to be treated. He held his head high.

When I left May Department Stores for Foot Locker, one of my first hiring calls was to Duane, who was assigned to mentor our executive trainees. He taught them well on a daily basis and offered good advice on their careers.

Duane had grace; he knew the Golden Rule and lived it every day. And along the way he helped a young, impatient, and grateful executive. He was a faithful employee.

✝ ✝ ✝

By his actions Jesus taught faithful employees how to handle themselves in difficult situations. He also modeled the ethics of a faithful employee. In the garden of Gethsemane, at great personal loss, he stood up for humankind. He did what he "ought" to do. He went forward on their behalf, never considering personal gain. God and his neighbors came first.

Near the end of the Sermon on the Mount, Jesus says, *"Enter through the narrow gate; for the gate is wide and the road is easy that leads to destruction, and there are many who take it. For the gate is narrow and the road is hard that leads to life, and there are few who find it."* (Matthew 7:13–14)

In business and Christian ethics, a critical word is "ought." What ought we to do? How ought we to act? Matthew Henry, the famed 17th-century theologian, comments on this concept of "ought" and this verse, by saying, "Christ came to teach us, not only what we know and believe, but what we are to do; not only toward God, but toward humankind. Not only toward those of our party and persuasion, but toward humankind in general, all with whom we have to do."

Jesus knew that taking the longer and narrower road was harder than to traverse the broad one, but it led to a shorter path of ethics. Each decision we make as employees in the marketplace carries with it an "ought." These "oughts" can sometimes bring terror or a reduction of personal gain. But Jesus says there is only one gate for an employee to enter. Employees who take the narrow gate help their companies in spite of the inherent risks that sometimes come from following this path.

✟ ✟ ✟

After my stint at Lord & Taylor, I was sent to another division called Robinson's Department Stores, where I met Lauren Peters. When I was first introduced to her, she thought she was having a friendly talk with the new person sent to help fix a broken division, but in fact she was being interviewed by me. I had been hired to help rebuild a broken staff. She had recently been hired as an internal auditor, fresh out of a large public accounting company. I knew I needed to find good people, and early on I talked in this manner with a number of potential helpers. I found Lauren eager, cooperative, and smart. She didn't know it at the time, but she passed the interview.

A week later, I visited our processing center for the first time, the center where we received goods and paid our bills. The manager was sitting on the floor behind huge piles of paper that needed sorting. I asked what he was doing. He said he was making sure the invoices matched what he received. *Why is he doing the work?* I wondered. He had a large staff and the requisite computers. Something else was wrong: Why was he doing his work on the floor?

Back in my office, I called Lauren's boss and said I needed her help. Her boss was stunned. "Let me get this straight: You saw an executive working on the floor and you think there's an accounting problem?"

"Yes."

"Maybe the problem's with you, but if you want to borrow Lauren, do so."

Lauren was also in disbelief that there was a problem. She was brand-new to retailing and didn't know anything about the accounts payable office. She said so.

"Smart people figure out complicated things," I told her. "Come back with your report in three weeks."

When Lauren returned three weeks later, she was nervous. "There's over three million dollars in accounting mistakes," she told me. This was a hard conversation for Lauren to have. I am sure it would have been easier for her to say there was nothing wrong. Certainly for the moment she would escape the drama that she knew would ensue. But she knew that an investigation would follow and that her findings would be challenged. She would be questioned from all sides.

She showed me her research. Wow! This was going to be hard to explain to the senior management team. She had discovered the reason the manager was on the floor. In the previous year, prior management, in an effort to inflate earnings, had removed information from the accounting system to improve profits. The manager working on the floor knew about this issue and had gathered up all the information himself and was trying to conceal the accounting discrepancy. Still, it had to be flagged. Management wasn't happy, but we were able to fix it.

I promoted Lauren and put her in charge of the Processing Department, not only because she had found the accounting error, but because she was honest and hardworking. She also had the cultural instincts I was looking for. Not trapped by tradition or the past, she was able to see more clearly. She was also able to approach her work with a warm assertiveness that got others to help her. She became well respected throughout May Department Stores.

As soon as I got to Foot Locker, I offered her a job. She accepted gladly. Years later, remarkably, she found the exact same accounting error at Footaction, a company we wanted to acquire, thereby saving Foot Locker huge embarrassment and money. She had the same look on her face when she found that mistake as she did years earlier at Robinson's.

Today, she is the CFO of Foot Locker. As a faithful employee, she uses the ethical path of "the narrow gate" in whatever she does.

Jesus was a good and faithful employee for God. Through the process of *kenosis* he gives us a model of how we can thrive and maintain our self-worth as a faithful employee in the marketplace. First, do our job. Second, do our job as if we are working for God, by adding value and achieving quality. Third, stay focused on God's will. And finally, do our job ethically by doing what we "ought" to do, in tough times and prosperous ones, with honor.

CHAPTER 5

JESUS, THE REPUTATIONAL BORROWER

"Go into the village ahead of you, and immediately you will find a donkey tied, and a colt with her; untie them and bring them to me. If anyone says anything to you, just say this: 'The Lord needs them.' And he will send them immediately."

–MATTHEW 21: 2–3

In the last week of Jesus's three-year mission he was near the village of Bethpage, at the Mount of Olives, about to enter the Holy City, Jerusalem. To fulfill the prophecy of Zachariah the prophet, so the Old Testament tells us, he was to enter Jerusalem on a colt or a donkey. He sent his disciples into the city to procure the donkey and the colt, a huge request in the first century, when livestock was precious, in many cases the center of a family's assets. The merchant who owned the animals readily agreed to lend them to Jesus. When the townspeople saw the disciples with the animals, they asked them why they were taking the donkey and the colt. To lend them to Jesus, the disciples explained. The townsfolk and the merchant knew Jesus and his reputation, and saw that this was right.

So begins the Palm Sunday story, which reveals the power of Jesus's reputation. The people and the owner of the livestock had heard about or knew Jesus, and how he had confronted the religious elite, who had used legalistic religiosity to control the marketplace. He was their hero. Jesus's reputation preceded him and was so strong he could randomly borrow a donkey and colt just by asking for them. The story underscores the importance of a strong reputation in our lives.

Jesus made friends in every town, in every marketplace. As he moved from town to town, he spoke with a variety of people. Some were poor, some rich; they were lepers, tax collectors, business owners, tradespeople, infirm or sound of body. He wasn't interested in any of that, or their heritage or philosophy, only who they were and where their hearts resided. By affirming their humanity, he generated goodwill. People could trust him because he cared about them. Jesus "did what he said and said what he did," allowing him leeway in his transactions. He didn't need to fill out extensive forms or sign lengthy contracts. Trust was enough.

When I left Foot Locker to become the CFO of Cushman & Wakefield—one of the largest and most respected companies in commercial real estate—one of my assignments turned out to be to help find a buyer for the company, which also meant establishing an independent source of financing. As our parent company would no longer be extending credit, I estimated we needed a revolving line of credit of $125 million.

I called not only on large banks, but on the relationships I had established at Foot Locker. My reputation was enough to get the banks to listen to our case, but that alone wasn't enough to *prove* our case. It took a lot of hard work to convince lenders that their investment would be solid. I had to show that beyond me, there were people of integrity at Cushman & Wakefield who could be trusted. Two executives, Mike Flood and Fran Clerkin, were critical in building this trust. With me, they produced the numbers to show that our need was appropriate and we had the money to pay the lenders back.

The work was hard for Mike and Fran, but the decision to say yes became easy for the banks that would be our largest lenders. Both men were honest and frank and worked hard preparing the backups the banks needed. They "did what they said and said what they did." The exchanges between Mike and Fran and the banks were collaborative and results oriented. When roadblocks were hit, solutions were created. When assets were needed for collateral, Mike and Fran would suggest a solution.

As the conversations progressed, a level of intimate trust developed between our group and the people representing the banks. Discussions would sometimes touch on the personal lives of the people at the table. Small clues showed that Mike and Fran were people the bank could trust—humanness in their family lives meant trustworthiness in business. The banks began to see in Mike and Fran what I saw; Mike and Fran began to see in the banks what I knew. Here was a negotiation that wasn't handled with cloak-and-dagger, but with frankness and transparency. Over time both groups developed trust for each other. Requests were completed with little need for debate. There was fellowship.

The deal was approved without fanfare. I was given far more credit than I deserved. Both sides succeeded because the people involved had hearts that could be trusted.

✞ ✞ ✞

In the last week of his mission, Jesus's disciples asked him where he wanted to have the Passover meal. In another example of Jesus's reputation preceding him, he sent his disciples to borrow a room for the Last Supper. Jesus said to them, *"Go into the city, and a man carrying a jar of water will meet you; follow him, and wherever he enters, say to the owner of the house 'The Teacher asks, Where is my guest room where I may eat the Passover with my disciples?' He will show you a large room upstairs, furnished and ready. Make preparations for us there."* (Mark 14:13–15)

Here he would hold one of his only formal committee meetings, a meeting where he would give instructions and lay out his disciples' future mission, for after he was gone. The owner of the house certainly knew of Jesus and potentially had had a conversation with him at some earlier moment. And Jesus's reputation was so strong he was able to borrow the room, now called the "Upper Room."

On the day I was made CFO at Foot Locker—then called the Woolworth Company—I knew sales were very weak and expenses were not being watched carefully enough. Someone told me that the banks wanted to rework our loan agreements. We were deeply in debt and they wanted a tighter repayment plan. Don't worry about it, I was told; it would be handled. Focus on the day-to-day and the problem would go away.

I knew differently. The banks obviously viewed the departing management with skepticism and would look on us the same way. Our managers had failed to meet the numbers they provided to the banks, and in some cases had been hostile. They treated the banks as a necessary evil and only complied when pushed. Unless I got personally involved, I felt, negotiations would not go well. The negotiations had to be completed in the next few days. I had to act quickly.

I wasn't secure enough at this point to handle everything by myself. I told my bosses that if I needed help, I would call on them. They agreed, but reluctantly.

Whom could the banks trust? I wondered. I did have an executive on my staff named Peter Brown, a quiet, unassuming man with an extraordinary combination of intellect and good manners, who had performed well for me in the past. Was he the answer? Peter had previously been slated to be fired, but I had interceded. Deep in the past he had worked as the assistant treasurer and thus knew the players. He knew what the banks wanted, and they knew he had come through for them in the past. His style was a forthright friendliness. "Under-promise and over-deliver" was his axiom. The banks trusted him more than they trusted our senior management.

I told Peter we needed to solve the bank issue in twenty-four hours and I was putting him in charge. He stared at me in disbelief. "Why me, why not John, our treasurer? I haven't been involved with this stuff for years."

"I need someone the banks know well," I explained. "I need someone competent, whom the banks could trust."

I also had done some math and knew we needed twenty-five million dollars in extra cushion. The plans I had been given by the company weren't realistic and weren't achievable.

"Let me get this straight," Peter said. "You want me to negotiate a new debt deal with the banks that don't trust us and ask for a twenty-five-million-dollar cushion?"

"You got it," I told him. "Remember: twenty-four hours."

Twenty-four hours later, Peter came to my office. "I don't know what you were worried about," he said smugly. "We have the deal you wanted."

Over the next year, we kept the banks informed of our progress, telling them the good and the bad. There were many close calls and sleepless nights. A number of times we came near the limits of the cushion, but we never exceeded them.

By the end of the year, it had become clear to the banks that their money was safe. Peter had guided us through this difficult period. Later he got promoted to treasurer and eventually became chief information officer. His reputation for being forthright, honest, and committed carried him well. He retired from Foot Locker in 2016.

Jesus borrowed because he could. Not just because he was the Son of God, but because he taught and lived lessons in relationships and partnering that built his reputation. All four Gospels describe the incident when he fed a large group of people with five loaves of bread and two fish. This story shows the power of Jesus's reputation in obtaining enough food to feed five thousand people.

When Jesus asked of Philip, an apostle, *"Where are we to buy bread for these people to eat?"* (John 6:5), Philip replied, "Six month's wages would not buy enough bread for each of them to get a little." Jesus was testing Philip to see if he had yet understood the importance of finding solutions and not roadblocks. Andrew, another apostle, thought a little harder and told Jesus about a boy who had five loaves of bread and two fish. Jesus told Andrew that that would be enough.

Jesus approached the boy and asked if he would share his bounty. Knowing Jesus's reputation, the boy agreed, thus innocently becoming the means Jesus needed for his next lesson. A young boy with very little, who knew Jesus's reputation and that good would come from his generosity, donated all he had to give. And from this generosity, Jesus was preparing the crowd to respond with their own acts of sharing—of their goods and their hearts.

He borrowed the bread and the fish, blessed the food, and had it distributed to the crowd. Everyone ate until they were all satisfied.

Jesus then told his disciples, *"**Gather up the fragments left over, so that nothing may be lost.**"* (John 6:12) They returned with twelve baskets of food, which they gave to the boy. He had given what little he had, but spiritually and physically he received back so much more.

Jesus had harnessed a community. He had given them confidence that following him was right. In turn, by sharing, they had contributed to the feeding.

Jesus could of course have created enough food without the help of the boy. He could have revealed his power to make miracles. But he was after changing the hearts of the people, from husbanding their possessions to being generous with them. Being able to borrow from the boy, who had very little to give, he showed the importance of a giving heart and the importance of having a strong enough reputation that a person with little in possessions would lend what he had, with a faith and trust that he would receive more in return.

Jesus asks that we follow and trust him. When we do, a satisfying outcome will be the result. Matthew Henry's commentary states, "Jesus can make a desert desirable." Jesus connects us to each other. His words and actions make us change our selfish ways to acts of generosity. We build our characters and our reputations.

At some point, we all have a FICO—Fair Isaac Corporation—score. It is reported by credit agencies, such as Experian or TransUnion, the companies that use the modeling system to predict how we will handle credit, and is essentially a reputation score. Surprisingly, it doesn't measure our net worth or our ability to pay our bills, but our *willingness* to pay, our reputation and what's in our hearts, to determine the FICO score.

The scores range from a high of 850 to a low of 300, which means the person is slow in paying bills and presents a poor credit risk. When we are consistently late in paying our bills, our score goes down, and vice versa. Any score of about 700 is considered good. No matter the score, it is there for all the world to see. When we have a bad FICO score, or reputational score. no matter how much our net worth is, it is hard to borrow. Jesus had few earthly assets, but he would have likely have had the highest score.

After Jesus's crucifixion, his reputation determined the fate of his human body, and during the period of the Resurrection he borrowed the remaining items to complete his mission. Two wealthy friends provided the material for his burial. Joseph of Arimathea assumed the main responsibility and provided the famous tomb. Nicodemus provided the embalming spices and helped Joseph with the burial.

A member of the ruling council and a wealthy merchant, Joseph had been a secret disciple, torn between the world of power and prestige and a heart searching for God. He knew Jesus was the personification of God, but he had remained in the shadows before the Crucifixion. When Jesus died on the cross, Joseph finally came forward and approached Pontius Pilate to ask for the body. Pilate agreed. Joseph claimed the body, covering it with a linen shroud he had just bought from a local merchant, and, with his compatriot Nicodemus, he buried the human form of Jesus. During the Resurrection, Jesus borrowed his last things in an earthly form.

Like Joseph, Nicodemus was a member of the ruling council. He, too, had been searching for God and earlier had engaged in secret conversations with Jesus. These conversations had led Nicodemus to believing and eventually loving God's Son. He had no doubt heard about the turning over of the tables at the great temple in Jerusalem, about the miracles and the healing. Over time, Jesus converted Nicodemus. In fact, Nicodemus was the first to hear two of Jesus's most important proclamations: ***"For God so loved the world that he gave his only Son, so that everyone who believes in Him may not perish but may have eternal life"*** (John 3:16) and ***"Indeed God did not send the Son into the world to condemn the world, but in order that the world might be saved through Him"*** (John 3:17).

Jesus did not start the conversations with Nicodemus with "believe or be doomed." He started by introducing ideas to ponder, and built his arguments at a pace Nicodemus could handle. Over time, Nicodemus was given the space to fully accept the message of Jesus and in turn was the first to hear Jesus's mission for humankind. Slowly and patiently Jesus pressed Nicodemus forward toward God, eventually arriving at a point of trust, a trust that led him to become publicly one of Jesus's final benefactors.

For both Joseph and Nicodemus, there was much to lose in following Jesus. Power, prestige, and wealth were all at risk. But over time, Jesus's consistent and trustworthy behavior convinced these two worthy men to stand by his side, perilous though it was. Jesus's reputation and his words diminished the importance of the men's worldly power and created two strong believers. Jesus instilled in them knowledge of the grace of God, and in turn they had acquired this grace for themselves. They provided Jesus with the last of his borrowed items, a shroud, the burial perfumes, and his tomb.

Jesus was able to borrow most of what he needed for his mission on behalf of God. Through his reputation people knew Jesus could be trusted and that their assets were safe with him and would serve a noble purpose. Jesus didn't borrow what he didn't need or use what he borrowed unwisely. The boy with the bread and fish, the owner of the donkey and the colt, the proprietor of the house with the upper room—they all knew Jesus by reputation, both as a human and as God. Each in his own way was paid back more than he gave.

In my business world Mike, Fran, and Peter were able to move lenders not just because they were good at their work, but because they were trusted and known to be respectful of those who lent their company money.

CHAPTER 6

JESUS, THE MODEL NETWORKER

"I can do nothing on my own. As I hear, I judge; and my judgment is just, because I seek to do not my own will but the will of him who sent me."

–JOHN 5:30

Jesus was the original networker, a master of facilitating productive and life-changing connections. He built his style around the concept of "with." In each interaction, he felt that his efforts worked in combination with those of his partners. Laborers, money changers, those in need of healing, etc., would benefit from his advice or performance when they participated with Jesus in solutions. And Jesus used these partnerships to expand his mission.

We see this use of a "with" activity in the Gospel of Mark, where Jesus is in Capernaum delivering his message to a crowd of people on the top floor of a house. Nearby on a mat outside the house lies a paralyzed man surrounded by four of his friends, who struggle to give the man enough space to be able to see the Son of God. Jesus is hemmed in on all sides; no clear path exists for the man's friends to get to Jesus. Undeterred and determined the paralyzed man and his friends head to the roof, remove some tiles, and lower the man to the floor in front of Jesus, where Jesus spots him.

Jesus says to the man lowered through the roof, *"Son, your sins are forgiven."* (Mark 2:5) The man remains still. Stunningly, Jesus does not heal the man yet. He has a deeper purpose. Jesus's words are heard by religious scribes. The scribes question in their hearts what they just heard, and begin whispering among themselves, conspiring to discredit Jesus, the world-changer. He has committed blasphemy, they charge among themselves. Only God can forgive sins. Their hearts are not open to God's message through Jesus. How can this man be able to forgive sins? They wish to retain their worldly status as those that direct religious thought. Jesus is threatening to upset this position.

Jesus overhears them. *"Why do you raise such questions in your hearts?"* he asks. *"Which is easier, to say to the paralytic, 'Your sins are forgiven,' or to say 'Stand up and take your mat and walk.' But so that you may know that the Son of Man has authority on earth to forgive sins..."* He turns to the man. *"I say to you, stand up, take your mat and go to your home."* (Mark 2:8–11)

The man stood, picked up his mat, and headed home. The crowd, amazed, realized that they had witnessed a miracle, an act of God, and no longer doubted that Jesus was the Son of God. He had healed the disabled man, and the faith of the man and of his four friends was rewarded by the healing. Jesus and the crippled man had worked together, an act that would help many in the future.

Jesus forgave the man's sins, in itself a remarkable act of compassion, for he saw a strong faith in the man's heart, but Jesus did more. He used the act to help soften the hearts of the religious scribes and to convince the onlookers of his divinity. By forgiving the disabled man,

Jesus let them question his authority, thus showing them that their hearts had been misled.

Jesus had seen the man's great faith through the man's valiant efforts to be healed. Jesus saw his need and healed. But Jesus also used the moment to establish who he was and his divinity. The man's persistence in trying to be healed was connected *with* Jesus's ability to heal.

In another instance, a woman waited patiently for Jesus as he was on his way to heal the daughter of a teacher at the local synagogue. When Jesus passed by her, she reached through the crowd surrounding him and touched his cloak. Having suffered for twelve years from hemorrhages, she had heard about Jesus's divine message and his many miracles. She knew of Jesus's divinity. Driven by faith, she knew she had to connect with him. She likely waited many long hours for Jesus to pass by. When he did, in one desperate attempt she reached through the crowd and found his cloak. This was all she needed. Just a touch would heal her and her misery would be swept away.

Jesus felt her touch and looked quickly to see who it was. In her eyes, Jesus saw this woman's great desire to be healed and said, ***"Take heart, daughter; your faith has made you well."*** (Matthew 9:22) She was instantly healed. She and Jesus shared a simple thing: by touching his cloak, the woman had shown her belief in him. The cloak had made them partners in faith.

The woman and the disabled man knew that Jesus could help, that he would change their lives in an instant. They didn't wait for Jesus to come to them; they both made heroic attempts to be healed. They weren't waiting for a genie to heal them; they both went to extraordinary efforts to connect with Jesus. For both, faith came first and the effort came second. And through their acts of togetherness *with* Jesus they were healed.

We see in these two great acts the essence of networking. In both cases, the individual had to find a person, Jesus, who could solve his or her problem. They both expressed faith that Jesus would be able to help, as is evident in their heroic efforts to find him. Then Jesus healed them. Without their act of faith, they would not have been healed. In both cases, they found unusual ways to connect with Jesus and approached him humbly. Their faith was expressed in their unusual actions. They didn't give up but searched hard for a way to get to the one, leaving to Jesus the act of solving their problems and releasing them to be closer to God.

✝ ✝ ✝

In fulfilling his mission, Jesus networked by traveling from Nazareth to Jerusalem to the Sea of Galilee and to dozens of small villages— thousands of miles and all with his feet. In an era when townsfolk would rarely venture thirty miles from their homes, Jesus's networking trips were extraordinary and very rare. His main goal was to "be with" the people, so they could become people of God. Mostly he met with those from the marketplace.

On these trips Jesus would often look for the people most connected to the community. In spite of their status of being considered one of the worst in terms of morality and business ethics, Jesus sought out the tax collectors. They generally knew everyone and everything; it was with the tax collector that Jesus could make the inroads he needed to make. When he found one with a heart for God, he connected.

A prime example was Matthew, who was a tax collector, but soon to be an apostle. When Jesus first met Matthew, he engaged him in a spirit-filled conversation. Jesus knew Matthew's reputation, but he also found a man tortured and tormented, a man looking for a new life and a way out of his existing circumstance. In Jesus, Matthew knew he had found the one. He immediately resigned from his job and started a new life.

Overwhelmed with the grace he had received from Jesus, Matthew quickly invited his friends and colleagues to his house for dinner to meet Jesus. Sinners and tax collectors showed up, representative of those that the Pharisees considered inferior.

But they weren't inferior, merely flawed. They knew their weaknesses and wanted a new life, and so they came willingly, in humility. Perhaps Jesus was the answer to their broken lives. Perhaps Jesus could lead them away from despair and emptiness.

"Why does he eat with tax collectors and sinners?" the Pharisees wondered.

Jesus had the answer: "*Those who are well have no need of a physician, but those who are sick. Go and learn what this means, 'I desire mercy not sacrifice.' For I have come to call not the righteous but sinners.*" (Matthew 9:12–13) Jesus knew that no ideal person existed, and he wasn't interested in those who thought they were perfect. He came to meet real people in their villages and houses. Jesus knew that the tax collector, properly righted, could provide a link to the masses desiring a new life.

The great twentieth-century theologian Dietrich Bonhoeffer voices the same idea: "God does not love some ideal person, but rather human beings just as we are, not some ideal world but rather the real world."

The Pharisees were proud of themselves. They knew the law. They knew the rules. They created the traditions that they demanded of society. They focused on sacrifice not mercy. They tried to be the most somber on the days of feasting. They wore their prayer shawls long so everyone could see how religious they had become. They knew everything but compassion. They knew how to judge, but didn't know that even those they considered vile craved forgiveness.

In the minds of the Pharisees sinners could only be prostitutes or thieves, but more likely they were actually everyday people who disagreed with the Pharisees and would not always follow their rules. These were the men and women with whom Jesus wanted to connect and network, ordinary people struggling to live and make a living. They were flawed but repentant, searching for a spiritual connection with God. Jesus didn't judge. He helped. He was a networker.

For Jesus, meals such as the one Matthew provided were an important means to reveal God's will and values, as well as a way to meet people who could connect him to larger groups. Jesus sought out people and people sought out Jesus. Networking.

I have a friend, Greg Rubin, who ran a successful consulting firm, SD Retail, for many years. Greg was a premier networker. He built his business on those he knew and those he trusted. He traveled the world, from Australia to Germany to England, and all fifty states, sometimes to connect to people he knew, sometimes to make new connections. His personal brand was his greatest asset. All who knew him trusted him.

During our difficult first days at Foot Locker we needed immediate help to streamline our organization, derailed by an inflated bureaucracy and archaic systems. We didn't have enough time for analyzing and dissecting all our flaws. We had six months at best and needed expert help quickly.

Greg to the rescue. We arranged a meeting to discuss our needs. Greg asked about our goals, probing for the problem areas. He asked for our timeline. I told him we had six months to fix our bloated cost structure and that we would have to work concurrently in all areas. Time was against us, I told him. The clock for our survival was ticking.

I told him, too, that I wanted the managers of the areas involved on board and that he couldn't provide any recommendations for change without the enthusiastic approval of those managers. Twenty areas needed to be fixed; I knew that without the cooperation of the individual managers, no plan would work.

Firms like Accenture and McKinsey had told me my time frame was unrealistic; also, their costs would have been more than we could afford. Besides, they would only use their methods, because that's the way their employees worked. They wouldn't bend and adapt themselves to our circumstances. So we turned to Greg.

His network told me Greg would have the answer. He came back after a few days and announced he had crafted a system that would meet our goals. It was a three-step process; he would have multiple teams working simultaneously. The first step was to ask the managers how they would start fixing their problems. Then Greg's team would establish an action plan with each of the managers. Many times what we think we want isn't the best solution. Greg would probe and investigate, providing better answers from objective research. Any disputes between Greg's teams and the managers would be resolved and sorted out. Finally, Greg's teams and the manager of the given area would meet with me, agree on the plan, and we would move forward.

We established a tracking schedule that was overseen by Greg's number two, Jim Sutliffe, and our internal guru, Mike Zawosky, and met weekly to monitor our progress. Mike and Jim wanted to make sure everyone was pleased, and more importantly that the managers of the areas affected approved of what we were doing.

Mike and Jim were the right choices because they possessed intellect and humility. They engendered trust. Our managers trusted them; Mike and Jim solicited their opinions and got straight answers.

The plan worked! We made the requisite changes in an extraordinarily short time. The internal managers, committed because they helped control the results, were proud of their accomplishments. Mike and Jim had managed egos and through a nonjudgmental approach kept the process flowing smoothly. Foot Locker saved millions of dollars and eliminated their stifling bureaucracy.

Throughout the next years I called on Greg for other projects and for information. He knew everyone and everyone knew him.

Greg never asked what was in it for him. He cared for the people he met and didn't offer his views without listening first. We became part of his network. He knew our spouses, our favorite sports teams, our preferred restaurants—and if we'd had some recent troubles. Sometimes he called with no agenda, just to stay connected. He wanted to make sure all was well at Foot Locker.

As a networker, Greg had earned the highest level of trust. His reputation was superior, and as does borrowing, networking requires a strong reputation. For Greg to be successful, people had to believe in him. If he made a recommendation, it had to work. His personal network was made up only of people he could trust. There had to be a history of success in his recommendations for him to remain successful. In today's marketplace, trust is the crucial element in our interactions with those with whom we work—bankers, vendors, or potential customers.

Networking is difficult; we have to be committed to solving the other person's problems as well as our own. We have to meet people where they are, like Jesus, often at meals. The people we help also have to be trustworthy and genuine. We must dig inside and listen to what the other person needs. Sometimes that can cause a short-term loss, but a long-term gain will result.

Jesus knew that networking was about giving, not getting. If he was to fulfill his mission—to save the world—he needed humankind. In John 5:30, he said *"I can do nothing on my own. As I hear, I judge; and my judgment is just, because I seek to do not my own will but*

the will of him who sent me." Jesus knew he needed to be a model networker to help people, who in turn could help his mission. Anyone was a candidate for his help, not just the rich and powerful, but also people on the margins.

Very early in his mission, Jesus was sitting alone at Jacob's well in Samaria. At noon, a woman showed up at the well carrying a bucket for water. Jesus asked her for a drink, seemingly a simple request, but the rest of the story exemplifies Jesus's approach to humankind.

The woman from Samaria had had a hard life. We can tell this from the circumstances under which she met Jesus. First, she was Samarian, and thus an outcast in the predominantly Jewish population. Also, she was a woman and therefore had few rights in the first century—many considered women nothing more than the property of their husbands. And she was drawing water at the hottest time of the day, rather than early in the morning when most women got their family's water, likely as a result of the other women of her community having rejected her. Yet here she was, the lowest on the social and economic scale, meeting with Jesus.

Jesus said, *"Give me a drink."* (John 4:7)

She was astonished: "How is it that you, a Jew, ask a drink of me, a woman of Samaria?" (John 4:9)

Jesus replied to the woman, *"If you knew the gift of God, and who it is saying to you, 'Give me a drink,' you would have asked him, and he would have given you living water."* (John 4:10)

Jesus did not want to discuss economic status or the politics of the Judean world. He wanted the woman to accept who he was, a path that would lead to marvelous things. But Jesus, the wise networker, was patient and proceeded slowly.

What does he really want? the woman thought suspiciously. But she didn't voice her question. Instead, she asked two different ones: "Sir, you have no bucket and the well is deep. Where do you get that living water?" (John 4:11) And "Are you greater than out ancestor Jacob, who gave us the well, and with his sons and his flock drank from it?" (John 4:12). The woman was forthright and curious, just what Jesus was looking for.

Jesus only partially answered her question with his reply, *"Everyone who drinks of this water will be thirsty again, but those who drink of the water that I will give them will never be thirsty. The water that I give will become in them a spring of water gushing up to eternal life."* (John 4:13–14)

Allowing Jesus to give her this water, rather than giving the well water to him, would lead her down a different path in her life. He was proposing a solution to her marginalized life, a solution that would release her from being rejected by her community and the greater Judean world. For Jesus, this would mean finding a go-between with the Samaritans. He still didn't answer her question of "Are you greater than out ancestor Jacob, who gave us the well, and with his sons and his flock drank from it?" He still had some work to complete with the woman.

The answer to her first question started to take her out of her understanding of the way her world works. How was it possible that water could come without a bucket? But Jesus wasn't offering physical water. Through an effective tactic of networking that involved providing a solution, Jesus was offering her a new way of life by connecting something familiar to her, water, to a spiritual life connected to God. Jesus was comparing an essential element of a physical life, water, to an essential element of a spiritual life, *living* water, meaning a relationship with God through Jesus. He was offering the woman an extension of her daily life, the inclusion of God. Like every good networker, he was giving, not getting.

The answer to the woman's second question is important historically. The woman knew the importance of Jacob and his connection to the Jewish faith. Jacob, the grandson of Abraham, was considered the patriarch of the Israelites. By asking Jesus if he was greater than Jacob, she was trying to discover his order in this sacred chain, she wanted to know his status in the history of her religious faith. The answer to this question would reveal if Jesus was genuine. She was still skeptical. A stranger has told you he has a better plan for your life. Why believe him?

Jesus didn't answer the last question immediately; he knew she was not ready. He first had to lay the groundwork to help her drink of the living water. His evangelistic style was to meet people where they were. He was not preaching, *Believe or be doomed.* Like a good networker, Jesus was working on the woman's own comprehension schedule, not his. He was, after all, connecting with a person made in God's image.

Jesus next revealed that he knew she had had five husbands and that the man she was living with now was not her husband. The woman was stunned. There was no way Jesus could have known about her past, but he did! She now knew Jesus was special. She called him a prophet. But Jesus replied, ***"God is spirit, and those who worship him must worship in spirit and truth."*** (John 4:24).

Maybe he wasn't merely a prophet, she thought. Wanting to learn more, she asked Jesus about the coming of the Messiah.

"I am he," Jesus responded, ***"the one who is speaking to you."*** (John 4:26)

The phrase "I am" is an important one in the Bible. It is the same phrase that God used to describe himself to Moses at the burning bush. It is how God described God to humankind. Upon hearing this, the woman was thrilled, and it at this point the Bible tell us she accepted Jesus.

Jesus finished the cycle. He had talked with her, networked with her. He was patient and led her slowly to the point of accepting his gift of living water. She had met Jesus, believed, and accepted His gift.

She hurried back to her home in Samaria to tell her neighbors and community leaders about Jesus. Hearing the woman's "Good News," they all rushed to Jacob's well, met Jesus, and asked him to stay with them for a few days. During Jesus's stay with the Samaritans, they discovered that the woman was correct in her assessment of him. The man they had invited into their world was God, the Answer. "We know that this is truly the Savior of the world," they declared (John 4:42)

Jesus completed his networking goal. Among other achievements he had converted a community in Samaria, a group who long ago had separated from their Jewish brothers. An extended community had crossed over to a new style of life, a spiritual life, based on one woman's referral and Jesus's networking style.

The woman received a renewed acceptance from her community. No longer did she have to go to the well at noon. She could now go with her community in the morning. She was freed. This community in Samaria was the first to accept Jesus en masse.

Jesus used the technique of giving and not getting in a conversation with just the right person, even though she was of low social and economic status. She was forthright, so Jesus could trust her. Jesus's gift of living water turned into a gift for an entire community.

✝ ✝ ✝

Jesus models how to build networks, and many times these networks become important when we need assistance. Overtime Jesus used these networks to facilitate his own mission. They opened doors. For those of us in the marketplace this is an important part of our working life. Building networks based on trust and fair dealings can help us in unexpected ways.

Part of my current advisory business is to help people find jobs. Usually, they come to me after failed attempts. They answer all the ads, go to a few interviews, and become frustrated and worried. "Why doesn't anyone want to hire me?" they ask.

When I meet with them, I often discover that they haven't used their network—those they know, those they have helped in the past.

A recent LinkedIn survey found that eighty-five percent of all jobs come through some form of networking. Other surveys agree: The majority of open jobs are filled through our connections.

Bill came to me after serving two years on a mission trip for the Catholic Church. Over sixty years old, he nevertheless wanted to reenter the job market. His field was compliance auditing, where he was considered an expert. He had superb references but still couldn't find work.

At our first meeting, I told him clearly that two factors were holding him back: his age, which he could do nothing about, and the fact that he wasn't using his network. He fumed at the age discrimination; it had taken him years to become the best. Over time, through our counseling sessions, Bill had to learn to accept the prejudice against him; no fix would make him younger or make the workplace change its bias. His only choice was to work harder.

Networking, however, was a method he could control, and he would have to learn how to tap into it as his best path to finding a job. At first he found it difficult. He was a naturally shy man and did not like to ask for favors. Each week I gave him an assignment: Contact seven people he knew well and let them know he was job hunting. Then contact seven people who knew *of him* to tell them he was available. Finally, contact seven people who had emailed or called him recently about professional issues. Twenty-one people a week. Bill didn't think he could find them, but after a few hours of hard work, he had his list.

I told him none of his calls or requests for help would succeed unless he was sincere in his approach. I reminded him to show genuine interest in his network and try to find out if there was anything he could do for them. He would be talking to people, I said, not just apple trees from which he needed fruit. He had to remind himself that the word "with" is a vital part of networking. He failed to find a job in the first week or second or third, but each week, with more and more difficulty, he constructed a new list and kept at his work. I told him that networking was like fishing: You don't catch fish unless your hook is in the water. The fish—and God—will come on their time, not ours, and you never know when. You have to go into a period of "faithful patience," when you network and when you work with God.

People you ask for assistance can't help unless there is a job open in their firm or they know of one. As they go about their business, they have lunches, talk with their colleagues, and circle around in their world. Ideas and jobs will emerge through these events. Unseen by the requestor, these conversations begin to swirl and take form. Perhaps there's a crisis and a prospective employer needs help immediately. Maybe someone is about to retire and a replacement will be needed. Many things may cause the fish to come, but fish and God will come on their own time.

The next few months were tough for Bill. He did his networking. He followed up in an appropriate manner (not too often so that people would think him a pest; just enough so that people would remember him). Lack of success made him discouraged. Sometimes he would call me for reassurance that he was doing everything he could. "It will happen," I would tell him. "Have faith." I had seen this many times, but for the person waiting, doubt is a natural companion. It is here that faith is important.

Not only would it happen, I knew, but it would happen in an unusual way. "Why are you so sure?" Bill asked. I replied that what he was experiencing was normal. I had seen it many times before.

One day, when I was out for a run, I got a text from Bill: "Call me. When it rains, it pours." Not only did one company need him, there were two. No longer did we discuss faithful patience, we talked about which job was best for his life and his family and what was God's will.

The two job offers were the result of different contacts. Two people from his network had referred Bill to people in need. The fish had come. His networking had paid off. His life now had a purpose, and he was able to thank God.

Jesus had a mission: to save the world. He couldn't do it by himself. His M.O. was to meet people where they were. He wandered thousands of miles. He met with the rich and the poor. He had countless lunches. He was always giving, and givers create long-term networks, because they look for solutions to help individuals. The people Jesus helped would work *with* him. Jesus carefully discovered these people and thus expanded his network.

CHAPTER 7

JESUS, THE SKILLFUL DELEGATOR

"After this the Lord appointed seventy others and sent them on ahead of him in pairs to every town and place where he himself intended to go."

–LUKE 10:1

By the midpoint of his mission, Jesus had healed many who came to him, performed a number of miracles, fed five thousand people, and established his senior management team, the twelve apostles. As he walked their land, many people, inspired by his preaching, joined him. Needing others to help, he added seventy people to his group of world-changers.

Seventy is an important number in Jewish tradition. Moses had seventy elders help him lead the Israelites in the wilderness. The ruling Jewish body, called the Sanhedrin, was seventy as well. Jesus's seventy were the nucleus of what would become a larger group, followers to expand his worldly mission.

It's easy to confuse the words "apostle" and "disciple"—both often appear interchangeably in the Gospels. The original apostles—John,

Peter, James, Matthew, and so on—were the first of the twelve who followed Jesus. Many others came later. They had heard of Jesus and wanted to help by following the teacher. The term "disciple" means "student" and the term "apostle" means "one who is sent." In many cases the followers of Jesus took on both roles: student and the one who is sent. While there is great debate about who and what they were, the seventy were a later addition to the band of helpers Jesus was assembling. Think of it as a middle-management layer of Jesus's blossoming organization. Essentially, this group of seventy were part of the group that would help Jesus "scale up" his efforts and earthly mission.

In time, many knew that Jesus was special. His listeners grew from one individual to adoring crowds. The word was spreading, and Jesus wanted more people to help him save the world and reveal God's values.

If Jesus was God, then why not save the world himself? Because God created humankind in his own image, as individuals not robots, and he wanted humankind to participate in this salvific act. Jesus could have used a business practice called "command and control," which needs no "buy in" from those commanded but generally produces only short-term results. Jesus chose instead to work *with* humankind, and God chose to reveal himself and his values and his love through Jesus. Through Jesus, he provided a motivated team.

God wanted to work in harmony with humanity, to act with their free will buoyed and influenced by the revelation of God's values transmitted through Jesus. Humankind, loved by God, was designed to work in relationship with him. We are relational creatures and abhor being commanded, but we love to and were created to work in concert with others. To completely succeed, Jesus needed to work on this level with humankind, those made in the image of God.

The numbers and opportunities kept expanding as the mission pressed forward, and Jesus turned to a management tactic called "delegation." He gathered up the seventy and sent them forth. He didn't say "just go do it." He gave them careful instructions, taught them what would work, and offered them advice. He armed the team with words of wisdom and lessons on how to be their best. He prepared them for success. He knew the way; he had been on the path before them and would be on the path with them.

In Matthew 10:16 we hear him saying, *"See, I am sending you out like sheep into the midst of wolves; so be wise as serpents and innocent as doves."* He knew there would be those who would resist change, happy where they were because they were comfortable in their power. But Jesus was proposing a radical shift that would be disruptive to the existing power base and way of life. No longer would the Pharisees have the final say on religious thought. No longer would the Sadducees control the temple and, in turn, the politics and commerce of the Judean world. Changes would be difficult for both groups. For others who resisted, the vision of a new life with God would arouse skepticism and doubt.

Jesus knew his band of seventy would face this resistance and intrigue. He warned his followers not to go about their mission naively. He instructed them to approach the resisters with kindness, that angry debate would achieve nothing. Rancor, he knew, would only delay the mission. He advised them to beware of resistance but to be positive to those who evinced it.

As the group was assembled, Jesus gave them a discourse on "Focusing on What Counts." Through the power of the Holy Spirit they would be able to heal many and to bring them to God. Some would accept, he told them, and some would resist. *"Whatever house you enter, first say 'Peace to this house!' And if anyone is there who shares in peace, your peace will rest on that person; but if not, it will return to you."* (Luke 10:5–6) The seventy would meet some who would accept Jesus's message and some who would not. With those that did, he said, they should continue; with those that resisted, they should move on. There was much to harvest and few to do the job of harvesting. He implored his team to be careful with their time. "Focus on what counts," he said and move with those who are ready.

Jesus had been on many of these trips before. He knew the pitfalls and how to surmount them, and he passed on his knowledge to the seventy, who would be carrying the brunt of the work from then on. He had built the prototype. For him to "scale up," the seventy would need to know the nuances of his success.

Jesus sent his disciples out with autonomy, but armed with their mission plan and teachings from earlier efforts. He taught them to fish so they could fish forever. He gave them the tools to be successful, including the Holy Spirit to help them on their way.

✞ ✞ ✞

In the lunchroom at one of my first jobs at a division of May Department Stores, sitting alone having lunch I overheard two women talking: One was a woman named Betty (I knew nothing more about her), the other a well-known character called Aunt Bea. Neither was in management and both were longtime employees who knew a lot about the company. They were complaining that the Display Department was no longer getting competitive bids for the purchase of materials and costs had gone way up.

"We used to pay a lot less for the whiteboards used in making the display signs," said Betty.

"I know," Aunt Bea grumbled. "And not to mention the costs for shipping them overnight to the stores. I wish they'd get their act together. They do things at the last minute. It's driving me crazy."

I introduced myself to them, explaining that I was in finance, new to the company, and wanted to learn more. Complaints poured forth: Standards had dropped, costs were rising, stores were receiving their signs behind schedule. The department was a mess. I asked for examples.

The next day they came to my cubicle to show me bills from the present and the past. I was stunned. Some of our costs were fifty percent higher. I went to a nearby store and asked how they felt about our service. Again, a deluge of complaints.

I met with the head of Display to discuss the situation. At first he was resistant, but finally he told me I was right, blaming the Advertising Department for the delays. "No matter how hard I try," he said, "they give me my work late. If I could get the material two days earlier, there'd be no problems."

So I went to the advertising chief. "We aren't getting input fast enough to comply with the Display Department's schedule," he said.

And so it went.

I laid out the problem to our CFO. He was surprised. "Okay, what's your solution?"

I suggested we ask the CEO if he could move up the advertising meeting by two days.

"They think that by keeping the schedule tight they can react better to sales trends," he told me.

"Maybe. But in actuality they're hurting sales because the stores can't physically act fast enough. They'll get better sales results with a more cohesive system, and we'll lower costs."

We presented my findings to the CEO. "Brilliant," he said. "I've been frustrated as well. We'll try your solution. Good work, Bruce."

I described my lunchtime meeting and told him that Betty and Aunt Bea deserved the credit. "We should give them a reward for caring about the company," I suggested. He agreed.

Two days later, the CEO and CFO called me into a meeting. May Department Stores, our parent company, had heard about Betty and Bea and had also been working on a way to get employees to submit their best ideas. They asked me to scope out something and get back to them. I went home that weekend and laid out a plan for my division. I used a term that had been floating around the corporation and referred to this new process as the "Profit Improvement Committee."

The process involved setting up a monthly meeting at which employees would present their ideas to senior management. Their suggestions were vetted beforehand by a financial executive whose only job was to work on the employees' ideas, eventually also making sure that the okayed ideas were implemented. In turn, the employee whose idea was accepted would get a reward.

There were conditions: The executive approving the ideas had to be open and positive. Negative comments would push people back into hiding. This didn't mean not rejecting bad ideas prior to these meetings; the executive could veto anything. But in the meeting, positivity had to abound. Second, the senior executive in charge of the idea had to "buy into" it before it was implemented. The division involved had to invest in having a financial executive coordinate the process. Finally, the employee reward had to be personal, engendering an emotional attachment between employee and company. A formulaic reward wouldn't do; we would lose the personal touch and the sense of real recognition. Later, in some divisions, we would give out movie tickets as well, so that the family could participate in what the employee had accomplished, thus engendering more positive reinforcement.

The process involved asking the employees of the company to help, to participate in process of making their company better. Instead of being told exactly what to do, they were given a voice. In effect, we were asking them "what do you think?" instead of expecting them to just come to work and do as they were told. It became a constructive way of hearing the silent complaints all employees have hidden.

Later, at Foot Locker, a woman who worked in our equipment repair depot suggested an idea that would save five hundred thousand dollars a year. She figured out that having spare printers in our stores would save on repair expenses. A broken printer could be repaired in a non-emergency situation, without the added costs that emergency repairs bring. Asked what she wanted as a reward, she said, "I'd love to take my children to Disney World." The company paid her expenses: ten thousand dollars for an idea that saved them half a million dollars. The family got to go on the trip of a lifetime. Word of this employee's success spread at Foot Locker and more ideas were generated, more disciples for the company created.

Within a year at May Department Stores, the idea developed during my weekend had spread to all of divisions. When I arrived at Foot Locker, I implemented the same process. And employees saved tens of millions of dollars for the company. Today, the process has spread to other companies well beyond my sphere. Foot Locker employees, transferring to other firms, took it with them, successfully.

The program succeeds whenever three principles are followed: The employees' ideas must be listened to in a positive manner. There can be no "gotchas"—collaboration among all is essential. The employees must receive a *personal* reward.

Critics will tell you that the employees are just doing their job, and they will want to add rules. Neither position is right; success is what matters. If the employees are listened to, they will do their jobs better, but they'll need autonomy. Rules wear cooperation down. Good people will succeed when they are heard, and most employees are good.

Today the process is called PIC, an acronym for Profit Improvement Committee. It works because it harnesses the power of humankind, and because the people who can effect change are assigned the task of change. It works because of its three simple principles. It works because it delegates authority to committed people.

Delegating intelligently increases a company's accomplishments. An employee feedback system like PIC gives employees a voice; collectively their voices become powerful. When employees have autonomy within a system designed to produce results, results will follow. While systems and autonomy are critical to good performance, the value for the individual employee of knowing he or she has helped is critical. The faith in the employee displayed by management is uplifting. It's the best aspect of delegation.

When Jesus delegated, he also picked great leaders, like the apostle Peter. After the Pentecost, where the Holy Spirit fell on the disciples and Jesus ascended to heaven, Peter assumed the leadership of the growing sect, called "The Way." In Peter's inaugural speech he reinforced Jesus's purpose, a message that both enthralled and comforted the crowd. After this message was delivered to a large crowd on his first day as leader, three thousand people converted to The Way. Each day more and more people joined, and Peter did a tremendous job recruiting and training this rapidly growing flock.

But wasn't this the same Peter who abandoned Jesus numerous times? The same man who seemed never able to grasp Jesus's message when Jesus walked the earth? The apostle who cowered in fear with the others during the dark three days of the Passion? In fact, as Jesus had predicted, Peter denied knowing him three times before the cock crowed in the early morning on the day of the Crucifixion.

Now Peter was the leader, the person convincing the masses of the rightness of Jesus's way. A new way to live. A new way to thrive in the marketplace. Jesus saw this greatness in Peter when it wasn't obvious.

A few years earlier, Jesus has said, *"And I tell you, you are Peter, and on this rock I will build my church, and the gates of Hades will not prevail against it."* (Matthew 16:18) Now Peter finally understood why Jesus had called him "the Rock."

Jesus had seen something in Peter. He changed his name from Simon to Peter. He announced that Peter would be the man to carry on his message. Yes, Jesus correctly predicted that Peter would deny him three times. He knew this, and still selected him.

Jesus spent time teaching Peter in spite of a multitude of missteps on Peter's part. He showed him how to move about the countryside. Peter learned that he could walk on water with faith. He learned that a few loaves of bread could feed thousands. Even though Peter failed many times, when it was his time, Jesus knew that Peter would be there. He knew that Peter was human like the rest of us, but special like few. He had delegated the mission of God to the right person.

✝ ✝ ✝

My daughter once asked me, "How many employees do you have working for you?"

"Thousands," I replied.

She was amazed. "It must be fun to have that many people to boss around."

"I don't boss them. I have to pay attention to them. I have to know how they're doing every day."

As a senior officer I was, in effect, mostly a marketplace social worker. Part of effective delegating is knowing another's strengths and knowing how each person is feeling. And then giving people responsibilities where they can succeed. Knowing three things about the people you are delegating tasks to is a critical aspect of management.

The first is their strengths and how best to maximize their gifts. The second is where they are less accomplished and what the ways are to minimize those weaknesses. The third and just as important thing to know is how people are doing personally. Are they upset about something or someone? Do they have quirks you have to be aware of? What are their emotional blind spots? Creatively adjusting our management styles to take these factors into account is an important part of effective delegation.

In 2009, in the middle of the Great Recession, the Yankee Candle CEO, Harlan Kent, asked me if I'd take on an employee named Reggie Thomas, who ran our Industrial Engineering Department. Reggie had become a troublesome employee according to HR and his boss. Trouble swirled around Reggie as he tried to implement change. As I evaluated him and his skills, I knew we needed his expertise in reducing costs. I had always liked Reggie because he was creative and proactive, though a little odd and in need of more than usual attention. I felt that Human Resources and his boss didn't understand his quirks, and that there was real human value in him.

I asked Reggie directly why he was considered a problem. He felt it was because he asked others for changes and this irked them. I knew some of the individuals involved and agreed they could be resistant. I went back to Harlan and told him we could make this work.

At the time the recession was hampering our sales and we needed to save money quickly. I felt that keeping Reggie rather than firing him would be a significant way to jump-start this process. Engineers like Reggie, who enjoy being creative, can be helpful, but only if they're given autonomy, trust, and a little extra personal attention.

At our first goal-setting meeting, Reggie started with low goals for expense savings and I started high. I felt that Reggie could save at least $10 million; he wanted a goal of $2–3 million. His number was the amount he was already saving. We needed more. He argued his limitations; I argued his potential. I told him his entire bonus for the year would be based on $10 million saved and asked him to come up with a plan.

He returned in two days with a smirk on his face, one I would come to see often. He told me he knew how to hit the $10 million mark but needed my support to help him with the resistors, a fair request for a tough goal. I believed he was capable and had a well-thought-out plan, so I agreed. What I didn't yet know was that Reggie, a special man, had special needs. Smart, insightful, and focused on what counted, he needed special approval all the time.

Each day that I could, I met with Reggie for ten minutes—only ten—to hear his plans for the day in reaching his goal. Mostly, I listened, usually agreed, and encouraged him, giving him a pat on the back and a willing ear. Harlan asked if I minded the frequent meetings. "All he needs is a headline and he's good for another day," I told him.

Delegating to people like Reggie, I tapped into three things. The first was autonomy. Creative people need the freedom to think. Too many rules and conditions stifle creativity. Second, creative people need to know they are contributing to a bigger goal that will produce a definable result. Third, they need an authentic statement of recognition. For Reggie this recognition came with his daily pats on the back and a sincere recognition of his value to our company. This was enough to propel him forward.

Thanks to Reggie, we got the $10 million. He knew his plan and he got support. The more successful he became, the more people followed him. There were no committees overseeing him, no rules to tie him up, just me and Harlan, also committed, moving here and there to help. He was delegated a job many multiples above his past performance. He finished his work because he had a purpose, felt appreciated, and was allowed to do his job unfettered.

There are three phases of management–new employee relationships that we all must pass through and desire to move through quickly: First, new employees are told *exactly* what to do. As they complete these tasks, they should be allowed to move on to the next level. In the second phase, new employees are told *generally* what to do. In this phase the employee is given more freedom and starts to anticipate the tasks that need to be performed. In the third phase, the manager asks "What do you think?" before the employee sets out on the job. This is the place most good employees want to be. This phase is marked by a mutual sense of confidence; the employee has shown ability and is given the freedom to determine how to complete his or her tasks. As managers, we must help employees get to phase three. It is in this phase that we unlock the creativity of humankind. But we must be willing to take risks and allow for differences of opinion. When we do, we can create a capable, confident, and productive employee. In Reggie's case, he quickly earned the right to be asked "What do you think?" Pressing in on telling him every detail of how to do his job would not have allowed him to accomplish his goal. He would have gone back to his desk and reluctantly done what he was specifically told, but the company would have lost his ingenuity and commitment.

In my current job as a business coach, I see this desire in everyone. They all want to be asked for their opinion. They want to be creative. They want autonomy and a sense of purpose. They want to be needed. Asking Reggie his opinion invigorated him. His creativity flourished. "What do you think?" is a vital aspect of delegation.

I've seen many managers who were perfectionists, wanting to control every step in the assignments they delegated. It's a limiting style, reducing the creativity of employees by sending the message that their ideas are valueless. They become robots, having learned to go along to get along rather than improve.

Such managers can be effective when it comes to small things, but their attitude limits their ability to achieve great results. Their employees' innate desire to do good, as well as their creativity, is suppressed. Loyalty to the company is surpassed by a simple desire to keep their jobs.

Controlling managers often operate out of fear, which makes them feel that they must dictate everything. The question "What do you think?" is lost, and along with it the greatness inherent in every individual, dooming those born in God's image to blind slavery.

✟ ✟ ✟

Part of being a good delegator is picking a team of people who understand the mission and can help achieve it. We do this by looking past résumés into individuals themselves. Asking five questions about the individual can lead us deeper into each of them. Can the individual get things done? Does he or she listen to learn? Can the individual develop and inspire others? Does he or she analyze effectively? Do they pursue success? If we can answer these five questions with a yes, we have a highly reliable partner.

As we begin to surround ourselves with people who can exhibit these traits, our cultures start to merge into groups of like-minded people. Culture is the most important determinant of a company's success, not the résumés. Like-minded people with the desire for success morph into an organization that can achieve great results. Delegation in this culture becomes an easy task.

Consider the twelve apostles. None was from the religious elite. Their résumés certainly did not suggest the future success they would have, but their hearts did. They all had to give up their lives to follow Jesus, who promised a different, riskier path that would burnish their self-worth. A life that gave them purpose. A life that conformed to their desire to help others. None came from a position of power, but they knew the people of the Judean world and had the cultural synergies Jesus desired.

And especially consider Matthew. Jesus met this tax collector after speaking to a large crowd at the Sea of Galilee. Matthew was sitting at his tax booth and Jesus wandered over.

"Follow me," he told the soon-to-be Apostle, and Matthew agreed. (Matthew 9:9) Remarkably, that's all it took. A simple request, an immediate acceptance. Jesus seemingly picked a random person to be his follower. But a deeper story lies behind this encounter.

Matthew lived his life torn between the terror of keeping his Roman employers happy and the fear of being cast off by his own people. Tax collectors for the Roman Empire were told to collect the taxes or else. Failure meant not only being fired, but imprisonment or worse.

Tax collectors were usually selected from the local population. They earned their salaries by over-collecting the taxes and abusing their neighbors to do so, creating a hostile relationship with those they lived among.

Matthew knew of Jesus and had heard his message. He realized he was on the wrong path, and his heart was unquiet. He recognized in Jesus a path to a different life, one that would free him from his unhappy trials and lead him to a life he had dreamed of in his youth.

As mentioned in Chapter 3, Jesus used tax collectors many times as examples for the marketplace. In the Gospels there are eight references to this much maligned group. Other than the occupation of shepherd, it is the most common occupation referred to by Jesus. He referred to it so often partly because he knew the Pharisees and others in power used his association with tax collectors as a way to slander him and his activities. Using the tax collector himself in parables and examples became Jesus's way of showing the redeemable nature of humanity. Even those in the most despised profession had value to

God if they possessed the right heart. Judging tax collectors eliminated seeing this value; getting to know them unveiled their hidden human value.

Jesus could have picked a Rabbi instead of Matthew. The Rabbi likely would have spent years studying the ancient documents and Torah. Created in his mind the ways of God. But would the Rabbi know people as well as a tax collector? Would the Rabbi have been an effective foil for Jesus?

Matthew set up a dinner with Jesus, his tax collector colleagues, and other friends, called sinners, suggesting a deeper commitment on his part than one would expect from a random meeting. By that time, Jesus had become a sensation. Matthew would have recognized what he was saying as pertinent to him. Besieged by Romans anxious for money and a community that usually shunned him when he appeared, he was open to change and Jesus offered it. The burdens of his life had overwhelmed him, and he gratefully turned to Jesus.

Jesus knew that Matthew had friends in the tax collector community, and it was Matthew's heart and connections that he wanted. Those Matthew had invited to dinner all showed up, their respect for Matthew evident in their attendance. He knew his own dilemma existed also in the hearts of his peers. He knew he was flawed, that that they were all flawed, and they wanted a way to change. By simply telling one man to follow him, Jesus had added people to follow his way. He knew Matthew was a key to a part of society others had rejected, that he was a thug by circumstance but an apostle at heart, and Jesus delegated to Matthew the task of letting Jesus fill the hearts of a rejected people.

Matthew wasn't a scholar. (As noted, none of the original twelve were from the religious elite. James and John had working for their father's fishing business; the others were people Jesus met in the marketplace.) The apostles were ordinary men whom Jesus could train to carry out his mission. All but one would have had yes answers to the five questions. Jesus moved from telling them what to do to granting them the autonomy of working on their own. Eleven of the twelve became great leaders after Jesus's ascension, and they formed the foundation of what was to become the greatest movement in human history.

✝ ✝ ✝

Another important aspect of delegation is knowing when you have to stop delegating to certain individuals and allow them to have a period of rest or Sabbath. In several of my management assignments, I had to become a social worker, ferreting out personal issues that affected an employees' ability to carry out their jobs. These issues were often externally caused—not the person's fault at all—but they impaired the employee's ability to work. We looked for such problems, and we often decided to protect a person whose success was under par, putting that employee in a shell that gave him or her space to recover.

At May Department Stores, I was aware of a woman (I'll call her Mary) whose performance had diminished over the course of weeks. She drifted off in meetings, her work suffered, and her smile had disappeared. I had been told in confidence that she was being subjected to spousal abuse. I brought her into my office to find out more. She initially denied there was anything wrong and promised to do better. I told her of my appreciation of her work and her value to the company. I was worried about her as a person, I said, eliciting a flood of tears. She relayed to me, her husband was abusive; she felt no longer safe as a person. The office was her only sanctuary, but she couldn't concentrate, given her fear of what would happen to her when she went back home.

I told her that her job—her sanctuary—was safe, and recommended she see meet with our Human Resources Department.

I assured her we would shield her until she recovered. The Human Resources Department, better skilled than I, provided the external resources to help Mary deal with her difficult situation.

As her situation improved, I noticed she would respond brilliantly when I asked for her opinion on a given problem. She regained her footing and her smile returned. Scars remained, but one day she sent me a thank-you note and we received back among us a person we could ask, "What do you think?"

Later at Foot Locker two men announced they needed open heart surgery. One was Bill Johnson, who ran our Communications Department and had heroically rescued our systems after 9/11. The twin towers had collapsed on our communications center, and for twenty-four hours we couldn't contact our stores or our other offices. It was Bill who found alternatives, and the following day we went live, while many companies were still recovering.

Larry Rinaldo, in charge of ensuring all our stores got their supplies on time, was the other heart patient. Each year, Larry did an outstanding job lowering our supply costs and improving our service. This hadn't always been the case with Larry. When he was first assigned to me, he was bureaucratic and slow. But just asking him "what do you think?' released him from the strict rules of a previously controlling manager. He flourished and his performance improved significantly.

Beyond their value as senior executives, these two men would attend our weekly meetings as my foils when I needed to make a point. They would accept tasks that other managers found too tough, and in private meetings they gave me honest feedback—not necessarily what I wanted to hear, but what I *needed* to hear.

Losing them on sick leave was going to be difficult. They had staffs that could cover for them, but without their brilliance, frankness, and energy. In the next few months, I called them weekly, not to discuss work, but to find out about their recoveries. I would tell Larry that Bill was recuperating more rapidly, and tell Bill that Larry was making better progress. My aim was to inspire each of them to get well quickly. They began to call each other and quickly discovered my ruse and began playing practical jokes on me as they were recuperating.

A couple of months later, they returned to work in the same week. They knew my game and their roles, which was to serve as examples for others. And I had back two employees to whom I could delegate difficult tasks and who would always tell me what I needed to know.

✟ ✟ ✟

Jesus never gave the disciples something to do he wasn't willing to do himself. Often this proved to be the hard road. He knew it wasn't a matter of simply commanding others, it was also describing the nuances of what it took to be successful, and laying out the challenges and hardships to be faced.

Luke 10:1 describes his method: *After this the Lord appointed seventy others and sent them on ahead of him in pairs to every town and place where he himself intended to go.* He himself had been rejected by the community of his youth, who saw him as no more than a carpenter from the marketplace. Too, the religious elite, fearing their loss of power, tried to trap him into making a mistake. They consistently probed for Jesus's weaknesses. Jesus knew where those carrying on God's mission were going and steadfastly backed them. Jesus had built the prototype for his mission and now he was ready to scale it up.

His past successes were magnificent. He had cured a woman who had hemorrhaged for twelve years. He had cast out demons. In a boat he had calmed a storm. He had inspired five thousand people to share their belongings and fed them all from five fish and two loaves of bread.

He had walked where the seventy were going. His followers knew he was willing to walk the same course he had asked them to take. This was the group that would be delivering the message without Jesus being present. Part of scaling up requires a well-informed group with similar values as the leader. Jesus knew the path and knew the seventy were ready to be independent. Through them the mission would get larger. As in any business that wants to grow, like-minded people were essential.

Jesus gave the apostles authority over all demons and the power to cure diseases (Luke 9–1). Apostles and disciples were armed with both the power of the Holy Spirit and the knowledge of Jesus's experiences. This wasn't merely a delegation of responsibility. It was a passing on of the torch that contained the passing on of authority. In scaling up, the group that follows having the same authority as the leader is critical to success. Merely sending out the seventy without that authority would have led to disaster. The disciples didn't have to check back for every little decision and be hemmed in by bureaucracy. They were free and trusted to do their job.

At Foot Locker, we recruited heavily from Penn State. Our recruiters would descend on the university, and through interviews and discussions with the professors they would find the best the school had to offer. The students we selected didn't just have the best grades, but also the cultural bias and attitudes we were looking for in future leaders. These graduates would be brought into a training program and rotated throughout our company. Our goal was to have them become skilled managers within three years.

I met with them frequently after they were hired. They were asked to complete a project and prepare a presentation to me. "Don't make a mistake," they were told. "Bruce will pick it up very quickly."

One at a time, a group of anxious new hires would come to my office and hand me their work. I would spend a few minutes going through it and, inevitably, find an error. Stunned, the newcomer would review his or her work and acknowledge the mistake. "They told me you had an amazing ability to spot mistakes," a fearless and forthright woman, named Heather Fodor, once said. "How did you find it?"

"I've done the same work many times," I told her. "I know where to look."

I explained the importance of experience that came from hours of doing what they had been assigned to do. Then I would show them some techniques to help them in the future. The process wasn't meant to embarrass the young executives, but to help them become armed to do their best job. They would be better able to embark on a road of independent work and produce better results than I could have achieved on my own.

Most of the "newbies" became "oldbies," going on to bigger things at Foot Locker. I'm sure they remember their first meetings with me and how nervous they were. Those meetings opened their eyes to the bigger missions in store for them. And we knew that we, their guides, had already been where they were going.

Jesus created the model for delegation, as is evident from the remarkable growth of his Way, now called Christianity. Jesus looked for the right people he could assign the tasks of growing his organization. He taught while he was delegating. He didn't use dictatorial management techniques, he asked "what do you think?" He got to know those he sent forth and helped them learn the nuances to be successful. He was willing to walk where he was sending his flock.

CHAPTER 8

JESUS, GOD'S CHANGE AGENT

*"He said to them, '**Cast the net to the right side of the boat and you will find some.**' So they cast it, and now they were not able to haul it in because there were so many fish."*

–JOHN 21:6

Many of the people who worked in the Judean world lived on the margins. Jerusalem, their base, was under constant threat of Roman conquerors, who could besiege them at will. In the first century, there were about 200 million people in the world, and much of what is now Europe and the area surrounding the Mediterranean Sea was controlled by the Roman Empire.

Only seventy-five percent of children survived their first year of life; half survived until the age of ten; life expectancy was around thirty. Few people had more than their daily needs; prices on the marketplace varied by multiples on any given day; food shortages were common in the cities. Existence was hard.

And it was hardest for women. Many were married around the age of twelve, often through an economic arrangement. They were considered the property of their husbands and had few if any rights. To become a widow was a sentence of poverty, with no means of support or protection.

There were no police, firemen, or EMTs. People defended themselves; sometimes neighbors provided assistance. They were ruled by local Roman centurions or officials, who in turn were helped by the compliant local political and religious authorities.

To make their quota, tax collectors could stop average people on the street and demand payment for what they were carrying. The fruit you bought the day before could cost three times as much the following day. Disease and illness had few cures; a minor infection could mean death.

Terrorists existed. They were called *Sicarti*, or "dagger men." They might murder their opponents in the middle of a crowd, then slip away unnoticed.

The temples were not like our churches of today. They were centers of commerce and politics, housed in a "sacred" building. The political and religious elite controlled commerce, politics, and religious thought. The wily rose to the top and often became like modern day thugs.

At the time of Jesus's mission for God, two prominent men ruled the temple under the sanction of the Roman Empire: Annas and his son-in-law, Caiaphas. Annas had been removed as high priest in AD 15, but remained one of the region's most influential political and social leaders, and his son-in-law was named high priest. They controlled the politics, commerce, and religious activity of the great temple of Jerusalem, and no activity within the temple happened without their knowledge. With their authority they kept the ruling

Romans comfortable and controlled the locals though their interpretation of the ancient Scriptures.

For them, the temple was a great commercial franchise. Each year, most of the Jewish population, many from the city but also from a larger group of neighboring communities, visited the temple three times, for Passover and other religious rites. Sacrifices were made during all three visits.

The temple had many rooms and courtyards. One room was reserved only for the priests, while the others were for those who made the pilgrimage, places where they could provide their sacrifices: money or livestock. The courtyard adjacent to the temple was called the Courtyard of the Gentiles, where one could exchange money at rates favorable to the priests and buy livestock at high prices.

To feed their family for that day, many rose early to go to the markets and sell their wares. Women would rise around dawn and go to the wells to get water to meet their families' need of that day. Children might or might not go to school. If they didn't, they worked helping out their parents. Each day as sun set, families would retire to their homes, exhausted from the labor of the day and the burden of sustaining life.

This was the world Jesus entered, a hand-to-mouth world of marginal existence where death from violence or disease lurked every day. He arrived in human form to effect a process of change.

Change to right the injustices of the world. Change from a marginal existence to a life of purpose. Change to upset the power structure. Change to the way the marketplace worked. Change to reorient the disoriented. He was a revelation from God in human form.

In human form, he had worked among these people of the marketplace for fifteen years. He had become a *tekton*. Like his human friends, he had struggled to survive. Surely he had visited the great temple of Jerusalem. He would have brought sacrifices and exchanged his money. He would have known the abuses that yoked the people to a marginal life. In living a life like theirs, he built an authenticity that would later help in his three-year mission to change this world.

The temple was no longer a sacred place for pious Jews, but a place used to take advantage of a pious people. During the last days of his mission, an angry Jesus entered the temple with some of his followers, made a whip out of cord, and drove out the merchants of the temple who were taking advantage of the visiting pilgrims. Protected by his followers, he sent those selling cattle, sheep, and doves into the streets.

He poured the money changers' coins onto the floor and over-turned their tables. *"My house shall be a house of prayer,"* he announced, *"but you have made it a den of robbers."* (Luke 19:46)

The temple merchants had paid huge franchise fees for their tables in the temple. The ruling body, led by Annas and Caiaphas, had learned how to use the temple for amassing personal wealth. The people knew they were being duped, but there was no other way; they were resigned to the abuse and paid up. The same people who were stealing from them controlled religious thought and demanded they come to the temple. This was no secret; everyone involved knew the game. The shills knew how to steal and protect themselves; they had a monopoly.

With the help of his friends, Jesus altered the paradigm. At great risk to himself and his followers, he exposed the corruption of the temple, he stated the truth. Jesus provides us with a model on how to effect change in the marketplace and our lives.

After World War I, conditions in Germany—inflation, the lack of a stable currency, social unrest, an inferiority complex, corrupt minis-ters, the need for scapegoats, and so forth—led to the rise of Adolf Hitler, who bombastically promised a better Germany under his rule.

Many Germans bought his message. They wanted the simple solutions proposed by this demagogue who used fear and violence as his mantra and vowed vengeance on the powers who'd defeated Germany in the war.

Into this atmosphere emerged Dietrich Bonhoeffer, a young and charismatic Lutheran theologian who fought against the simplistic slogans Hitler preached and urged his countrymen to resist. Ordained at the age of twenty-five in 1931, he warned at St. Matthews, the Lutheran church of Berlin, the religious hub of Germany that neither St. Matthews —nor Germany itself—would survive Hitler. Bonhoeffer was imploring Germans to make a change that would correct the course of an impending disaster.

On January 30, 1933, Hitler ascended to power. Two days later, Bonhoeffer went on national radio to urge Germans "not to slip into the idolatrous cult of the Führer." In mid-sentence, he was cut off the air. Later, Hitler would assume control of the Lutheran Church and install a Nazi sycophant to run it. He would also secure an agreement from the Vatican not to interfere in German politics.

In response Bonhoeffer became one of the founders of a new and competing church called the "Confessing Church," set up specifically to oppose Hitler's assumption of power over the religious institutions of Germany. Hitler would later close the Confessing churches down and arrest many of their clergy. Bonhoeffer retreated to America in 1939 and became a professor at Union Theological Seminary in New York City. Bonhoeffer remained unsettled in New York and felt guilt leaving his country and his role as its national change agent. After much internal debate he returned to Germany. "I have come to the conclusion that I made a mistake in coming to America," he said. "I must live through this difficult period in our national history with the people of Germany. I have no right to participate in the reconstruction of Christian life in Germany after the war if I do not share the trials of this time with my people." He returned to his homeland on the last passenger boat to cross the Atlantic.

Because of his fame, the Nazis let him live, but he was forbidden to speak in public. He became part of a group whose aim was to assassinate Hitler, but he was caught and sent to prison. His spiritual advice was sought not only by the other prisoners, but by the guards as well. Less than four weeks before the end of World War II, he was executed. His executioner said his death was more peaceful than any he'd ever seen.

Bonhoeffer, the change agent, knew Hitler would be responsible for the deaths of thousands of sons in Germany, throughout Europe, and America. He saw an alliance with evil resulting in the death of morality and the destruction of the country he loved.

St. Matthew's Lutheran Church, the most important Lutheran church in Germany, where Bonhoeffer was schooled, was, as predicted by Bonhoeffer, heavily damaged by Allied bombs, but Bonhoeffer's voice from its pulpit still resonates throughout the world. He became one of the most published theologians of the twentieth century, and his solo cry is still an inspiration. To act as change agent in the face of overwhelming odds can be costly, as it was for Jesus and Bonhoeffer, but change agents are vital to society and the marketplace.

When we consider our own corporate failures, we wonder who will preach change. What if one person had stood up at Wells Fargo? we wonder. What if one person had said no to BP? Jesus surely would have. So would Bonhoeffer. Both were examples of change agents who saw the need for change based on what was right.

Change agents avoid the encumbering philosophy of "go along to get along." They know that chronic crisis will inevitably blow up into acute crisis. Jesus showed us this. Bonhoeffer listened.

Even for us, who do not have to stand up to Hitler or the degradation of the great temple of Jerusalem, our workplace lives are filled with dilemmas and moral questions that require new perspectives. We must learn to be like Jesus, to see things not as they are, but as they should be.

In a late scene from the Gospels, Jesus gives us another model for making changes in our business perspectives.

Peter and six other disciples were at the Sea of Galilee, a large lake north of Jerusalem. Peter decided to go fishing one night and invited the others to join him. They fished the entire night without success; not one fish was caught.

By this time, Jesus had been crucified, risen, and appeared two other times to the disciples. He was now walking on the shore at daybreak and called out to the seven, *"Children, you have no fish, have you?"* (John 21:5)

"No," they replied.

"Cast the net to the right side of the boat and you will find some." (John 21:6)

Peter was a professional fisherman. James and John, sons of a man who owned a fishing company, were in the boat as well. They were experts. And here was Jesus, a carpenter, giving them advice on how to fish! They respected Jesus and loved him, but was this his field of expertise?

Still, all seven disciples said, "Why not? Our way hasn't worked."

They cast to the right, and quickly filled their net, which grew so heavy that they couldn't lift it into the boat and had to drag its contents to the shore. One hundred and fifty-three fish were in the net! Simply by changing their routine and casting to the right, they produced different and better results.

What did Jesus know that they didn't? Had he seen a swarm of fish on the right side of the boat? Was Jesus creating a miracle to demonstrate God's power?

Once again he had asked the experts to reject the tradition of their process when things didn't work out. Try a different way, look at the problem from a different angle. A small change in perspective may create a bounty. Be open to change was Jesus's lesson. The fish were there, but the old methods needed to change.

✝ ✝ ✝

In the early months of 1999, when Foot Locker was on the verge of bankruptcy, my staff and I tried to find ways to lower the company's expenses. We worked hard to keep our struggling company afloat with innovative ideas, and each week we met to discuss our progress. By early summer, I had begun to notice fatigue in our group. The ideas had virtually run out. One mistake by us and we were finished. But each time we thought we had nothing more to find, this resilient group found ways to complete our tasks.

I had to give this fatigued group a message: "Regardless of where we are and regardless of our circumstances, we have no option but to continue to try."

I knew that our Sales Department was working hard. I saw it in their impassioned meetings. *Their ideas will work, we just have to buy them more time*, I thought. In the third quarter, on our last day, we were $300,000 away from making our goal. We couldn't let that stand, we needed one more push. I made everyone stay long into the night to find the money.

Then it happened, into my office came our head of Corporate Accounting, Giovanna Cipriano, and a longtime employee from our Treasury Department, Nancy Herman. They told me they had found an obscure item that would keep us alive: a utility deposit that had expired but could be brought back. We survived, but things didn't improve during the early part of the fourth quarter. As we entered the Christmas season, our sales still weren't responding. It was our lowest point, the furthest away we had been all year. I had resisted calls for almost twelve months to prepare for a bankruptcy, even though our CEO wanted it. We had a job to do and that was where we should stay focused, I insisted. But sales needed to change.

On December 24, 1999 I finally called our lawyers at Skadden/Arps and told them to be prepared for a bankruptcy filing. I set January 6, 2000 as the day of decision. Things looked bad and we needed a miracle. Peter Brown had suggested January 6 to buy us a little more time, and I agreed.

Three important sales projects that we'd started in the summer would quite unexpectedly emerge during this twelve-day period. At best these ideas had been large gambles, but now they had to pay off. They were driven by unusual people who looked at our problems in a different way: They looked to the right.

When I came back on the 26, I noticed an anomaly in our sales numbers. They were heading up by more than ten percent! I'd seen similar spikes before and was suspicious, but the following day when I came into the office, sales continued going up. Perhaps this wasn't a head fake, maybe this was real. And so it went. By the sixth of January, instead of filing for bankruptcy, we were trying to find out how big the sales shift was and what it meant for our future. The crisis was passing and we were going to survive. Not only survive, as it turns out, but start to thrive.

Earlier in the year, three significant changes had been made to our sales-generating effort that created this after-Christmas sales surge. Our "goal line stand" in keeping the company alive had bought the company enough time for them to take effect. I had seen them develop in the sales meeting during the summer and they were implemented just in time.

In the second quarter of that year, Lauren Peters had suggested selling gift cards in our stores to help with post-Christmas sales. Initial efforts with a vendor had shown promise. "Let's try it," I told her. "What do you need from me?"

"Convince marketing that it's a good move."

Not an easy task. Marketing was resistant. What could finance types know about sales? they must have thought. And how were we going to pay for this?

Even though I was the finance chief, earlier in my career I had run sales departments at previous jobs and had a good idea of what worked and what didn't. Ultimately we convinced Marketing to try, mostly by agreeing to pay for the experiment and to do most of the work.

Gift cards don't help your sales before Christmas, but after Christmas. Recipients use them to buy your products, potentially having a positive impact on sales. Thus Foot Locker became one of the first retailers to have a national gift card program. The hard work paid off at the register after Christmas.

But gift cards weren't the only factor that lifted our sales. Nike and our sales team had noticed that vibrantly colored sneakers were selling well in selected markets. Tim Finn, the president of our U.S. division, had found buried in our product inventory a style of sneaker that Nike could use in its successful Air line (designed around Michael Jordan). Tim brought the idea to Matt Serra, the future CEO of Foot Locker, and with Matt's support got Nike to agree to produce the sneaker. The new sneaker was called Tuned Air. It wasn't ready until late December, but when the new shoes hit our stores, they sold and sold, to the tune of three million pairs by the end of the first year.

Matt himself had a third solution. He had a well-earned reputation as a skilled merchant, and more than anyone else changed the course of Foot Locker. He felt that our promotions were strong but lacked a special message. Before Matt, the merchants had always looked at extra promotions as detrimental to our image, but Matt reached into his past experience at department stores and created for Foot Locker a new marketing event—BOGO—"buy one, and get one at a discount." Many in the company were dubious it would work, but I was all for it because we would turn our products faster, and while the percentages weren't as good, the dollars came quicker. "We pay our bills with dollars and not percentages," I told the doubters.

Matt implemented his program, and it produced better results than even he had dreamed. Customers no longer looked at Foot Locker as a stale and staid company. Our promotions had vibrancy and sparkle. Matt changed the way we fished. He helped us learn to start casting to the right.

We survived that year, even while enduring headlines in *The Wall Street Journal* calling us a "financially troubled company." Over the next year we got accustomed to beating sales every day and speculated on how high we could go. In 2002, in an article by *Forbes* magazine, our efforts were praised. We were no longer the "financially troubled company," but a robust company, leader in its field, called Foot Locker. Random posts by others on my LinkedIn profile page say that I was Foot Locker's savior or that I was a great change agent. Past colleagues also call me a change agent and thank me for all I did. These compliments are essentially inaccurate. I was actually a *facilitator* for great change agents. All I did was give them the space to be change agents. What is true, though, is that I was lucky to work with great teams and had a bulldog persistence in helping them succeed.

As a senior manager for most of my career, I learned how to spot good change agents. They see the world in simple terms and don't get hung up or rely on tradition. They don't think about their personal gain, but only about succeeding.

Change agents ask, "Why don't you cast to the right?" Thy thrive when they have autonomy, not detractors. They aren't always the shiniest penny in the company or the ones with the most impressive résumés, but they think differently and know what is possible. They aren't clanging noisy people, but insightful people who proceed without personal fear. With one change, they can alter events, filling a net with 153 fish.

When there's a crisis, we should look to the change agent. Small changes, tweaks, and simple additions are often all that we need. When bigger change is needed, listen to the radical ideas, the new approaches, partner with the agent, and plunge ahead.

Jesus changed the ancient world. He stood up to the corrupt power of those running the Lord's house. He showed people how to be connected to God. He changed the way the Lord's house was used. Like all great change agents—and Jesus was the greatest—he focused on what was right and showed us that "casting to the right" works. Great change agents like Dietrich Bonhoeffer and my colleagues at Foot Locker emulate Jesus's style. They aren't hemmed in by tradition, can see a different future than the masses, and are focused on the right way to do things. In the marketplace, companies like Foot Locker need to constantly change the way they do business. New technologies and ideas are their conduit to change. Companies that move forward thrive, those that don't drift away. When we work with God and see life as it should be, we emerge into a self-determination that is connected to the Almighty.

CHAPTER 9

JESUS, THE PERFECT SALESMAN

"For the Son of Man came not to be served but to serve, and to give his life a ransom for many."

—MARK 10:45

Jesus was the world's greatest salesman, and what he was selling was a relationship with God. He did it by partnering: listening first, prescribing afterward. No quick fixes, no panaceas. "Turn to God" was too simplistic an answer for most problems, though of course it was ultimately *the* answer. He would show his followers a specific course of action built on the teachings of God. His technique worked. From nothing, he built a connection between God and humankind that today has two billion followers.

Consider what he accomplished in just three years. Helped by twelve apostles who gave up their careers to follow him, he created the world's largest company, an organization whose primary focus was on "doing good."

He convinced a foreign woman at a well, rejected by society and her own community, to bring his message to her nation. He found seventy people to deliver his message throughout the Judean world. After the Resurrection, his apostles cemented a way of life to follow. Later, his teaching would be carried throughout the Roman Empire by the apostle Paul, and ultimately Christianity became the state religion of Rome in the fifth century. Jesus touched many hearts and changed many lives, and he did it through serving, not being served. *"For even the Son of Man came not to be served but to serve, and to give his life a ransom for many,"* he said. (Mark 10:45) His main focus was to find solutions to humankind's ills, and to show that he cared. The "hard sell" was not in his lexicon. He knew he had solutions and that he was put on earth to show others the way.

"How many cars a month does your best salesperson sell?" I asked my friend Tom, a finance manager for a large automobile dealership.

"Over thirty," he replied.

Wow! Even if he worked six days a week, that was almost a car and a half a day. Amazing, when you consider the paperwork, customer service, and follow-up he would have to accomplish.

"How does he do it? What's was his secret?

"Referrals and repeat customers," Tom laughed. "He has built quite a following."

He built it carefully: Birthday and anniversary cards to his customers, notes asking how the car was running and if there was any-thing he could do to help, occasional inquiries on how the kids were doing in college—all gentle reminders that he was available to them, that he cared. When customers came in, he asked what they needed and told them what he had to sell. He didn't try to push his most prof-itable cars, but advised the customers on which car was best for *them*.

His customers knew he could be trusted. He respected them, affirmed their humanity. He built his clientele slowly, taking the long road and the narrow gate, not the easy one. People would come in and say they wanted Tom, not the next salesman on the floor. His bosses gave him difficult customers because he knew best how to make them happy. In three years, he was the dealership's top salesman. He cared about solutions. If only briefly, he entered their lives.

Jesus knew that selling wasn't just about finding solutions, but also about carrying the solutions out. His healings and miracles demonstrated that he could do what he promised, and that he cared about each person he helped. His recruits knew from others that a touch of his cloak or a brief encounter was all they needed. They knew that people could rely on him, that he lived up to his promises. Besides finding solutions, Jesus completed his work with quality.

Bobbie Ridgeley was the Executive Director of A Future with Hope, an organization providing help to homeowners recovering from natural disasters, like Superstorm Sandy. She was an effective manager, respected by the staff, the board of directors, and most importantly, her clients. The work she oversaw was completed on schedule; her people had the right solutions. Thanks mainly to Bobbie, A Future with Hope achieved the highest completion rates of home placements after Superstorm Sandy, over ninety percent. Bobbie became a sought-after spokeswoman by other agencies and fundraisers. All wanting to know how she did it!

I was chairman and president of A Future with Hope, and I asked Bobbie to help us fundraise along with her other duties. In nonprofits, fundraising is the sales function. You have to convince potential donors of the importance of the work and that their money will be spent wisely.

"I'm not a good salesperson," she told me. "I don't have personality and charisma. I'm not qualified."

She was right. She wasn't flamboyant, she didn't have the desire or ability to wow people with flowery words. She had an engineer's training and stayed riveted on producing with extraordinarily high standards. Her best sales tool was her ability to execute. Her goal was to help people get back into their homes, ones that were "Safe, Sanitary and Secure." Her staff knew that for her the homeowner came first and work had to be completed professionally. When the bills had to get paid, they were paid on time. When donors needed reports, they were finished promptly and accurately.

However, she was also a great salesperson; she just sold by her deeds, not words. To help alleviate her concerns with her sales efforts, I took her to see Ken Alexo, then the head of development and fundraising for Drew University, where I had gotten my degree in Theology, and asked him to help her with concepts of how to raise money.

"Do things that create positive results," Ken instructed. "First, let the donors know you're their partner. Second, spend their money wisely. Finally, understand your donors' goals in giving and serve their purpose."

Bobbie was already doing all these things. Indeed, the American Red Cross considered A Future with Hope their most committed grantee out of the hundreds they sponsored. When the Robin Hood Foundation had extra money, they would often approach Bobbie. People would call her out of the blue to offer funds. She was selling with deeds and her personal brand.

What was her secret? She cared about her work and people recognized it. She had high standards and a strong code of ethics. She listened to learn and paid attention.

Bobbie achieved more than she would admit. A Future with Hope spent well over ninety percent of its funding to help people. Her completion rate was almost double the state of New Jersey's. She was a great salesperson, despite her belief that she didn't have the requisite charisma.

With the help of Bishop John Schol of the United Methodist Church, A Future with Hope raised over $17 million and helped out in more than half of the most difficult situations after Superstorm Sandy, allowing people to reenter "Safe, Sanitary and Secure" homes. Bobbie was selling all the time. She just didn't realize it

Great salespeople develop trust. They get to know their customer and that person's goals. They establish a link of common interests and demonstrate genuine concern. They execute their promises. A good salesperson cares about the apple tree not the apples. *Can I help?* they ask. Is there a mutual connection? They affirm the value of their customer as well as their own. They execute the solution as if they are working for God.

✝ ✝ ✝

What was Jesus selling? A productive relationship with God. Jesus wasn't selling Christianity in itself, but was urging humankind to follow a way of life designed by God. (In fact, the label of "Christianity" didn't come into being until many years after Jesus's ascension.) Jesus's first followers were looked on as a backwater sect of Judaism, and the movement was called "The Way," meaning a separate belief in the power of Jesus. It was only after Christianity had begun to spread outside the Judean world that it acquired its current label.

Jesus was selling a different way of life to help people, especially those in the marketplace, a set of values radically different from the norms of the first century. He sold God's values not through a hard pitch or for personal power, but through a sales approach that focused on the individual he was addressing. Jesus didn't use a "one size fits all" sales method, he connected directly with people and their lives.

He was extraordinary at connecting with those he was helping. *"Listen! I am standing at the door, knocking; if you hear my voice and open the door, I will come to you and eat with you, and you with me,"* he said. (Revelations 3:20)

An interesting approach. Jesus is waiting for us humans to let him into our lives, but he isn't standing at the door to give us a hard sell. He wants to be *with* us, suggesting a conversational approach, not a "believe or be doomed" method. He uses the vehicle of sharing a meal to get to know us; he's with us to converse, not for the hard sell. His purpose is to hear us first, and then for us to know him.

For this method to be effective, Jesus had to develop trust—trust that is developed over a cosmic meal. Clearly dining is a metaphor for his getting to hear us and our getting to know him. Of course, in Jesus's divine nature, he knows us already, but he also knows that he has to craft within us a condition of trust with him. Jesus knows that trust is built because we ourselves believe we are trustworthy. Jesus helps us arrive at this point of believing in ourselves through repentance and our accepting a changed life. An understanding that we are worthy of God's love, because we believe in God and our sins are truly forgiven. We begin to see ourselves as a creation made in the image of God. When we arrive at this spot, we can trust ourselves and we can trust Jesus with our story.

This view of Jesus supports the theory of a relational Christ. Jesus walks *with* us on our journey through life toward a productive relationship with God We must first trust Jesus, which is derived from a cosmic dining conversation with Jesus. We need to learn the meaning of the name *Emmanuel*, which means "God is *with* us."

After building trust and our faith, Jesus becomes a partner who helps solve the problems of life. In the story of the woman with hemorrhaging told earlier, we see Jesus's approach. She reaches out to him as he passes by through a large crowd. He turns. ***"Who touched my clothes?"*** he asks (Mark 5:30) His disciples ask, "How could you know who it was? The crowds are completely surrounding you." Jesus had spotted her cosmically among the many. He knew from her expression that she trusted him. ***"Daughter, your faith has made you well; go in peace and be healed of your disease."*** (Mark 5:34)

Many who read this verse assume that Jesus healed her alone, but her faith in Jesus helped heal her. It was a mutual act, for it required an act of faith on her part. She had trusted in God through Jesus. She knew Jesus would heal her, which is why she pushed through the crowd to touch his clothes, an act by a woman who, in the first century, would not ordinarily be allowed to get that close to a great teacher. Her touch released the power of healing. Jesus knew the solution she needed and completed the job.

At a different time, Jesus cured ten lepers. Leprosy was a dark curse in the first century, and lepers were put in isolated communities to keep them away from their healthy neighbors, who in turn shunned them out of fear of contracting the disease.

One leper, a Samaritan, approached Jesus to thank him and to praise God. Jesus said, ***"Get up and go on your way; your faith has made you well."*** (Luke 17:19) Again Jesus had healed not by his singular action, but by connecting with a person who believed in Jesus's solution. The leper knew it was God who had cured him. Faith in the Son of God was the answer.

Jesus tried to help everyone—not just the rich, the powerful, but also, importantly, the lowest of society, including a sick woman in a male-dominated society and a leper from a foreign land. Part of Jesus's sales technique was to be available to all and to shun no one.

Today, if Jesus were selling to a large company CEO, he would sell to everyone he met on his journey to get the big sale with the CEO.

He wouldn't ignore the little guy, quite the contrary. While he was in the reception area, he would get to know the receptionist. If he saw the warehouse worker, he would engage them in conversation. He would be selling trust to everybody. He would affirm the humanity he saw in all the people he met along the way. All would be respected. In turn he would get the sale.

Early in my career, I was assigned to get permits from the City of Los Angeles to allow us to have a liquidation sale in a few of our stores. Our parent company, May Department Stores, provided me with a high-powered lawyer to expedite the process. We went to the permit office. The lawyer told me to stay in the background and keep quiet, he would handle everything. He was cocky and confident. The matter would only take a few minutes.

The lawyer approached the clerk, explaining why we should get the permits. His arrogance set my teeth on edge. The clerk told him to take a seat. After a period of waiting, she told us that we hadn't filled out the forms correctly and advised us to come back in two weeks. The lawyer exploded. He was going to call the clerk's boss, the mayor, and if necessary, go to court to get satisfaction. The clerk was unperturbed. She had enlisted a fellow worker to bring back breakfast and she didn't cower when our lawyer threatened to have her fired.

I reported back to Corporate, who were upset and, like their lawyer, vowed to fight to the end. Without my superior's knowledge, I contacted an attorney friend of mine to ask if he could help. He knew the clerk and the process, and he came up with a plan.

He and I arrived the next day, just as the city office was opening. My friend said hi to the clerk and asked how she was doing. They knew each other and engaged in a quick "catching up" conversation.

The clerk noticed me. "Aren't you the man who was with the obnoxious lawyer yesterday?"

I acknowledged that I was.

They asked us to sit. Five minutes later, the clerk handed us the permits we needed. I went back to headquarters. "We don't need your lawyer," I told them. "I have the permits and we're good to go."

Stunned, they asked how I'd accomplished it. I told them I wasn't sure, but they owed my friend an hour at his billing rate.

Most salespeople are given a goal by management, and incorrectly they almost always begin to think about ways to reach that goal, but this should be the second step not the first. The first step should be figuring out what the right solutions and products are for your customers. It is here in this thought process that Jesus's approach helps us. Our first thought is naturally how to reach the goal. However, Jesus will tell us that it should be how we satisfy and provide solutions to our customers. Having to hit a sales number is not enough to make us effective; creating elegant solutions makes us effective.

Considering the recent Wells Fargo scandal, we see this flaw. The higher-ups created excessive sales goals for the salespeople and in turn demanded these results. In fear of losing their jobs, the branch salespeople began opening up accounts and issuing credit cards without the customer's knowledge. All to hit an unrealistic sales goal.

When the news hit the press regarding this practice, Wells Fargo, once considered one of America's best banks, went into a nosedive with many repercussions. The CEO resigned in disgrace, the bank lost a significant amount of stock value, and over five thousand people were fired. What if they had started with *What do our customers need?*

Jesus knew his sales goal, and his "manager" was God. He also knew he had to find elegant solutions to sell his way. He had come to earth to save human beings, to offer hope to those hemmed in by a difficult life. He became a redeemer, a go-between between humankind and God. His goal was to convince humankind of what he was selling, and to succeed he had to provide solutions to earthly problems by using God's values.

If you search on Google for "The Book of Signs," up will pop the Gospel of John. The Gospel of John is many times referred to in this manner. It contains seven signs or miracles of Jesus. Included are familiar stories like the feeding of the five thousand, the resurrection of Jesus, and the raising of Lazarus. All signs that point to the divinity of Jesus, miracles that provided solutions. Some scholars believe these signs are part of a *New Creation Theology*. The signs are a critical message in the Gospel of John and are contained in chapters two to twelve. The first of these signs/miracles is the turning of water into wine, which starts at the beginning of chapter two.

Jesus had been baptized and had gathered up his first twelve disciples, called the Apostles. Jesus was just starting his three-year mission. He was at a wedding in Cana, a town in Galilee. The guests had drunk all the wine before the festivities ended and wanted more. Mary, Jesus's mother, also a guest, asked Jesus to help. Here it was, a chance for Jesus to provide a solution to his customer, humanity. A solution to show Jesus was the way and the truth. A way to help create his reputation as a solution provider.

He told the servants to fill six stone jars with water. Each could hold thirty gallons. The servants did as they were instructed. *"Now draw some out, and take it to the chief steward,"* Jesus said. (John 2:8)

The steward tasted the water. Miraculously, it had changed into wine. Not just any wine, but the best wine. The steward congratulated the bridegroom for keeping the best for the end of the ceremony.

In the first century, weddings were large events attended by most of the bride and groom's community. To save costs, the bridegroom and his family normally would serve the best wine first and save the cheaper wine for later, when the guests were too drunk to notice. "Everyone serves the good wine first, and then the inferior wine after the guests have become drunk. But you have kept the good wine until now," the steward told bridegroom in John 2:10. Word spread through the crowd that it was Jesus who had provided the solution. "Jesus did this, the first of his signs, in Cana of Galilee, and revealed his glory; and his disciples believed in him," the Gospel of John writer tells us. (2:11)

Jesus didn't just sell, he *did*. In doing so, he convinced the crowd that he was selling a solution, not just any solution but an elegant solution for his customer, with a better than normal result: fine wine. He had revealed his glory and who he was. Jesus had started achieving his sales goal, not with fancy words but with a simple act of problem-solving to help a bridegroom out. His first thought was providing a solution.

As Foot Locker got healthier, we began to attract people who wanted to sell us their services. We now had money to pay our bills, and people knew it. Peter Brown, who had previously created an elegant solution with our banks that helped save Foot Locker, and I were asked by a bank representative, one of the few we didn't entirely trust, if we could give him time to make a sales pitch. Since others from the bank had been helpful to us during our troubles, we agreed.

The representative suggested we buy back some of our stock— which, incidentally, would earn him a large commission. Peter and I felt that we could get a better return on our cash by investing in the growth of our store base and expanding our e-commerce business. Our board backed us. We showed the numbers to the representative.

"This doesn't help me earn my bonus," he blurted. "You have to do this deal or I'll lose my bonus."

He wasn't interested in the best solution for us, but in hitting his sales goal. Peter and I were surprised by his candor. His plea also contained a veiled threat that if we didn't help him, the bank would not be as supportive the next time we needed its help. While we continued working with the bank, we began a transition toward other banks we felt had more mutual interests, not just theirs.

Later, when I was serving on boards, when that representative's name came up I suggested that his interest wouldn't be aligned with ours. We moved on to other banks.

Jesus developed a great following, among them great salespeople. Even after his crucifixion, he made sure his followers understood their mission. He appeared to the apostles and disciples three more times and told them what a good salesperson for God should do. Peter, his closest apostle, continued forward. Peter and the others remained riveted on spreading the word throughout the Judean world, performing miracles and healing the sick. They continued Jesus's practice of selling solutions, not their personal sales goals. They made The Way a strong local sect. But Jesus wanted them to expand.

Opposing them was a staunch enemy of this sect: a man named Saul of Taurus, who was a tentmaker.

Some say Saul was a well-trained member of the ruling Sanhedrin, educated by some of the great leaders of the Jewish faith. He reviled the people of The Way and led the effort to persecute the movement's members. In an effort to prove his worth to his mentors Saul traveled throughout Judea to search out followers of The Way and have them arrested. Saul erroneously believed that with this zealotry he would prove himself and satisfy his desire to be a man of God.

Jesus had other plans for him. He had one more post-crucifixion appearance to make and one more salesperson to create: Saul.

Saul was riding to Damascus with a group of fellow zealots to bring followers of The Way back to Jerusalem for trial.

As they were riding, light from the heavens flashed above Saul's head and threw him to the ground. He heard Jesus's voice: ***"Saul, Saul, why do you persecute me?"*** (Acts 9:4)

"Who are you, Lord?" Saul asked, knowing immediately that it was the voice of Jesus.

Saul had furiously searched all his life to discover who God was. He was a premier scholar of the ancient Scriptures and an upcoming religious star. He was determined to prove to his cohorts that he was worthy of their respect, and so he hunted down people who believed in Jesus.

However, deep inside of him his study of the Scriptures had not provided the answer, nor had the zealot's education satisfied him. This empty search for truth had now been exposed by Jesus. Lying on the ground, blinded by light, Saul was about to find the answer he had long searched for:

"I am Jesus, whom you are persecuting. But get up and enter the city, and you will be told what you are to do." (Acts 9:5–6)

Saul's search was over. We notice in Saul's first response to Jesus that he recognizes the divinity of Jesus, when he says, "Who are you, Lord?" In a moment of heavenly intervention, his life was changed and his zeal was satisfied. He realized he had seen the face of God. The very person he was attacking was his solution.

Jesus's friends led Saul to Damascus, a place where he could learn how to spread The Way. But, still blinded by the light, he didn't eat or drink. Meanwhile, Jesus spoke through a vision to a local resident named Ananias, himself a follower of The Way, telling him to go to

Saul and help him. Ananias knew of Saul's reputation as a persecutor. Could this really be Jesus who had spoken to him?

Jesus answered: ***"Go, for he is an instrument whom I have chosen to bring my name before Gentiles and kings and before the people of Israel; I myself will show him how much he must suffer for the sake of my name."*** (Acts 9:15–16)

Jesus was about to spread his word internationally by using Saul. As a reference point, the "Gentiles" were considered to be anyone outside Judaism: Romans, the Greeks, the Samaritans, the Persians. Jesus knew who Saul was. Yes, the persecutor of The Way, but a man with many fine qualities, enough to be one of Christianity's great salespeople.

What did Jesus see in Saul that he was about to give him one of history's greatest sales jobs? For one thing, Saul was committed to the pursuit of excellence. No matter how hard anyone else worked, Saul worked harder. He had studied the Scriptures and, though still young, had risen to the top of religious scholars. Too, he was fearless, having survived many near-death experiences. He would travel anywhere, endure any trial.

Saul was also from the marketplace. He was a tentmaker and had learned how to sell his wares to his community. He made his tents in Tarsus, a Roman outpost on a significant trade route, and it is likely Saul learned in this spot how to be *international*.

Because he was a Roman citizen and had learned the ancient Scriptures, Saul could read and write at least four languages—Greek, Latin, Aramaic, and Hebrew—at a time when most people were illiterate. A remarkable skill, when we consider that in the first century, spaces did not separate words. For instance, "See Dick run" would be written "seedickrun." Hebrew was even harder, for it contained no vowels and was read right to left. In Hebrew the same phrase, "See Dick Run," would become "NRKCDS." Saul could preach in the four languages he knew and was for this and other reasons the right man to spread Jesus's lessons. He was a scholar and a tradesman. Perfect.

Ananias approached Saul. "Brother Saul," he said, "the Lord Jesus, who appeared to you on your way here, has sent me so that you may regain your sight and be filled with the Holy Spirit." (Acts 9:17) Immediately scales fell away from Saul's eyes and his sight was restored. He was baptized, ate, and regained his strength, a convert to Jesus and to God. And about to become Jesus's best salesperson.

But like most who convert after a lifetime of searching, Saul was too eager. He tried to spread The Word clumsily and created enemies through his zeal. In Damascus for his own protection, he was lowered over the wall in a bucket and told never to return. He met similar resistance in Jerusalem. Jesus then sent him to the Arabian desert, a place where he could gather himself and reflect on his mission. There he stayed for three years.

Saul changed his name to Paul, a name that would be familiar to the Gentiles and the Roman Empire. He rid himself of the excessive zeal that hampered his ability to listen. He transformed himself into a salesman of Christianity, a man who listened and looked for solutions.

As Paul, he embarked on three great sales trips. He traveled throughout the Roman Empire and set up Christian churches in Greece and Turkey. Persecution was rife, and Paul's travels were difficult. Fortunately for him the Roman Empire had constructed roads that were safe. Vandals and thieves had lurked at every corner of the trade routes that used to be where Paul was now walking, before Rome captured most of the territory surrounding the Mediterranean Ocean and Europe. Ironically, the roads constructed by the persecuting Roman Empire made Paul's journey easier as he spread the Word of Jesus.

Still danger lurked. In some towns he was beaten and imprisoned; but in others, the people listened. Like the original seventy disciples, Paul healed many of the sick and used Jesus's methods of listening for solutions and spending time with those who were anxious to learn from him.

On one trip, he traveled to Athens, the center of philosophy and art in the first century, a place where great minds met and exchanged ideas. Because of Paul's reputation for eloquence, he was invited to speak at the Areopagus, a rock outcropping in Athens, a place where great philosophers of the first century spoke. Even though the Greeks had many gods, Paul took this opportunity to deliver a great sermon and suggest a solution.

He delivered his fullest recorded sermon from this spot, not admonishing his listeners to change their beliefs, but recognizing their desire to be connected to God. "Athenians, I see how extremely religious you are in every way," he said, pointing to the many statues of Greek gods that surrounded the promontory. (Acts 17:22) By affirming their desire to know God, he used one of the important things a good salesperson should learn to do: He showed them respect. They became more receptive to his message.

He pointed out that a local altar had been dedicated to an "unknown god" and told the crowd that it was the God they were seeking. (Acts 17:23) A God they did not know. He told them the history of Israel and the coming of Jesus and his salvation.

The Athenians were riveted. They had struggled for years to define God and had fragmented him, erecting statues of his many facets. It was the unknown God they were seeking, Paul explained, and they need look no further. This statue, among the many, was the symbol of an undefinable God, a God who had always been in their midst. Not all Saul's listeners were converted, but many understood his message; he had established a foothold for Christianity in Greece, today the center of the Eastern Orthodox Church.

Like any good salesperson, Paul continued to follow up with those he met and kept the dialogue going. Thirteen books of the New

Testament contain the letters that either Paul wrote directly or that were attributed to him in the communities he visited.

Paul's sales mission took hold. Jesus had found a tentmaker from the marketplace to carry on his message. For the next three hundred years, the message survived and spread. Despite frequent Roman persecutions, Christianity became embedded in the Roman Empire.

Paul's letters and works became the foundation of what was to become an international religion. In the fourth century, when Constantine assumed power, he had the story of Jesus. As he was preparing for the Battle of the Milvian Bridge, he saw a vision in the sun, a cross of light. He told his soldiers to adorn their shields with this cross. He won the battle, and attributed his success to the light of the cross.

Soon after, Constantine legalized Christianity—in effect, setting up the foundation for Christianity to become the state religion of the Roman Empire and later the Holy Roman Empire, the religion of a vast part of the world. Jesus's Way had evolved from being a backwater sect of Judaism to being the religion of billions of people around the globe.

A zealous tentmaker from the marketplace learned the ways of Jesus's approach to selling and became the great earthly salesperson for Jesus.

In the early fifth century, after the fall of Rome, Jesus's Way was kept alive by Christian monks, living in monasteries, who maintained the faith and its writings. Through a dark period, lasting almost one thousand years, the embers of Christianity continued to burn.

During the Renaissance, great teachers with new ideas further expanded Jesus's Word. In Germany, Martin Luther introduced the concept of writing the Bible in local languages along with Greek and Latin, providing local populations with Jesus's teachings.

Saints of the Catholic Church emerged, such as Ignatius of Loyola, a former mercenary, who was given a Bible while recovering from a war wound and became a tireless promoter of the faith. He created over five hundred Christian schools in his lifetime, and even today many colleges owe their roots to Ignatius.

In the seventeenth century, Christianity spread even to North America. It continues to grow in Africa, the Philippines, China, and south of the equator.

Jesus the salesman founded a way that was connected to God and spread it throughout the world. A way that allows humanity to have a relationship with our creator. A way that is so universal it survives every cultural change and invention. It survives because Jesus's way is about finding solutions and working with humankind.

Contemporary culture will shift and continue to shift, but Christianity will be part of life as long as its fundamentals—its moral code, its lessons of love God and your neighbor—remain.

CHAPTER 10

JESUS, BUILDER OF UNUSUAL TEAMS

"What is born of the flesh is flesh and what is born of the Spirit is spirit."

–JOHN 3:6

No great company, no great business, no great executive can function without a committed team. To form a team, executives study résumés, ask others about each prospective team member, conduct interviews with every candidate—and decide whom to hire.

Often, these methods aren't enough. As mentioned earlier, there are five questions that should be investigated when considering a candidate for employment. They are:

- Can the prospective employee get things done?
- Does he or she assertively pursue opportunities?
- Does the candidate know how to listen to learn?
- Can he or she analyze data effectively?
- Does the candidate know how to develop others and inspire other team members?

If we can answer yes to these questions, then we have a potentially strong employee. Further, if the candidate is also warm and assertive without being overbearing, and desiring of achieving ethical and focused results, we have a person we should hire. The answers to these critical questions aren't on a résumé, they're within the candidate and must be discovered.

Jesus built a team, and in eleven out of twelve cases he chose correctly. They were committed to God and Jesus's message. He could have picked the most learned rabbi, but he did not see fidelity to the values of God in the existing clergy leadership, rather he saw individuals trapped in the lure of their own power and tradition.

So Jesus picked ordinary people from the marketplace, those who were willing to give up everything for God and God's ideals. Jesus was the Son, and his choice was limitless; he used a set of criteria unique to his mission. Attitude was crucial—there were no "superstars" or egos to deal with. In ordinary people he saw potential for great success. His choices were able to focus on the future, not the past, and they understood the masses because they were from the masses. They were open to new experiences, new ideas. For this mission they weren't encumbered by their status or traditions. They were free to see things as they should be and not as they were. Class, wealth, and education meant little to Jesus; other people's opinions meant little to him. He didn't spurn the rich—witness Joseph of Arimathea—but he concentrated on ordinary men and women with extraordinary souls.

Early in my career at May Department Stores, I was taught to look for the five human qualities, described above, that promised good employees. It was a lesson us younger executives were given almost daily. Great leaders like Dave Farrell, the long-serving CEO, and Jerome Loeb, the president, pushed it down through our organization on an almost daily basis. We all became aligned to these principles and they created our culture.

This became evident in all my transfers to other divisions. I always met people with similar values and the same commitment to success. At each stop, I worked with warm, assertive people who got things done, developed others, analyzed effectively, pursued opportunities, and listened to learn. Going to new assignments was easier because of these shared values. Our culture was strong, and May Department Stores was considered the best run retailer for decades.

In every assignment I admired my bosses. They cared little about their personal interests and listened to learn. They didn't promote themselves; they wanted knowledge.

They strove to make their peers and subordinates better at their jobs, by giving guidance and, once the lessons were learned, freedom.

They were good analyzers, able to look at problems or opportunities objectively. They didn't pre-judge before they had the facts, and they sought solutions that would help the team and the company.

They approached people with respect and warmth and were almost always positive and rarely hostile. They remained committed to doing a good job ethically.

Their "to do" lists were completed on time. They focused on what counted, disregarding their personal agendas. They had no time for distractions.

When I first got to Foot Locker, I needed to find friends quickly who had these same five characteristics. But I had to be careful in my approach. It's easy to come into a tough situation and announce you're going to change everything; easy to be disparaging of the past, your employees, and your predecessors; easy to think you know the answers without the full set of facts at your disposal. But that's the wrong approach.

I discovered it was easier to find out what was already working and look for current employees who could help, on the theory that it's easier to make progress with allies than with enemies. Joe Bongiorno, Peter Brown, Peter Cupps, and Mike Zawosky had all had considerable careers at Foot Locker before I arrived, but all had been largely overlooked by their superiors. When I talked to them, I found they had the five qualities of good employees. I merged them with people I knew from my own past, like Lauren, Kevin, and Marc, and we developed a team that promoted the message of the company and avoided self-interest. When we found employees who exhibited these shared traits, we labeled them with a term we developed, "profile employee," meaning they had the requisite five characteristics. They worked for the company, not themselves. Everyone we thought of hiring or bringing into our circle was evaluated. If the candidate was a "profile employee," we brought that person in. If a candidate didn't possess the five traits, he or she was ruled out.

Our circle soon expanded to form a powerful group that could work on its own, for our values became the culture. The culture worked because we weren't trapped by tradition or hemmed in by our personal status or power. For Foot Locker this group became the team that held the goal line when things looked the bleakest. We survived because of these common values.

Jesus knew that in building teams, success depended not only on hiring the right people, but on training those people to live up to their God-given talents. He recognized that all people have blind spots to go along with their gifts. Jesus concentrated on maximizing people's strengths, while minimizing their weaknesses. Sometimes the effort was simple, other times intense. The aim was always to help the team become more effective and live into their mission.

Jesus had his own mission and the team to fulfill it. While touring the countryside, he looked for people to help—not just anyone, but those who listened to learn, those who accomplished what they set out to do, those who were warmly assertive, those who could develop subordinates, provide solutions, and analyze effectively.

As we've seen, he found them in the marketplace. Some needed freedom to move forward, others needed blind spots removed. One who only needed freedom and had limited blind spots was Matthew, a well-connected tax collector, who would open up to God's will the world of those mired in sin. Matthew was a self-starter who thrived on autonomy and encouragement to get Jesus's mission accomplished. I've told you of the dinner Jesus attended at Matthew's house.

For me at Foot Locker that individual was Joe Bongiorno. Joe had been mired in a place of unfulfilled potential. Not by his own doing, but because people missed the greatness in this man. Perhaps he was too humble. Perhaps he walked too softly. But he always did his job with the five characteristics as his guide. As with Matthew, all I had to do was tell Joe what needed doing and he always surprised me with his ingenuity in getting the thing done. When Joe took over our supply chain, the situation improved immediately. There was little fanfare. It just got better. Weekly update calls with Joe were short and to the point. Things got done and Joe earned the respect of all those who worked with him.

Jesus knew the same about Matthew. He was well connected and had an authenticity that would attract his friends to the famous dinner. He knew also that Matthew was dedicated to helping him, because of his Jesus-granted release from an unfulfilled life. With little fanfare Matthew did his work. The critical dinner was an example of Matthew just getting the job done and doing so without drama. From that dinner many saw a new way and changed their life's direction. In turn, they began to help spread the divine news.

Peter, a well-regarded fisherman, became Jesus's appointed successor. Peter was bold, a leader, and willing to speak his mind. But he had a blind spot Jesus had to resolve: Peter was not completely committed to The Way. He often wavered back and forth. He would abandon Jesus at times and other times never quite seem to get the message.

But Jesus saw greatness in him, and as with all fine art, Jesus saw that with a little chiseling around the edges Peter could live into his potential. Jesus hung in there with Peter, when many would have been frustrated and given up.

After Jesus had risen, he met his apostles and disciples one more time for breakfast. After this breakfast Jesus pulled Peter aside. *"Simon son of John, do you love me more than these?"* he asked. (John 21:15)

Peter sat in amazement. He was, he knew, looking into the eyes of God in human form and being asked if he loved this human God more than "these." Not just the friends who had traveled with Jesus and Peter for the last three years. Jesus's question was in fact more profound: Would Peter supplant all his worldly desires to follow the way of Jesus? It is the same question Jesus asks us in the marketplace. Are we willing to supplant our personal ambitions for ourselves, our company, our fellow employees, and follow the path of Jesus?

"Yes, Lord; you know that I love you," Peter replied, to which Jesus said, *"Feed my lambs."* (John 21:15)

Jesus asked again, *"Simon son of John, do you love me?"* (John 21:16)

Peter still did not fully understand that Jesus was trying to remove him from his past, nor did he know that Jesus wanted him to relinquish everything he knew from the world to carry forward the mission of God.

Peter replied, "Yes, Lord you know that I love you."

Jesus asks a third time, **"Simon, son of John do you love me?"** (John 21:17)

What am I missing? Peter wondered, feeling frustrated and hurt. He dug within himself to find a response that would satisfy Jesus while he wrestled with the thought of "these." He realized that Jesus *was* pressing him to give up his world and become fully and completely part of the mission of God. There could be no compromise. He had to move from being interested in following God to being *committed* to following God. Across the table, Jesus the Son of God was staring at him. There was no escape.

"Lord, you know everything; you know that I love you," Peter said. He did not use the word "yes," and now simply answered using the word "Lord," showing a committed acknowledgment of Jesus's divinity.

Jesus now accepted this answer and told Peter of the struggles the former fisherman would have to endure, pointing out that Peter's future would be filled with many successes, but he would have to give up his worldly ways and eventually be put to death. Jesus accepts Peter's answer and says, *"Follow me."* (John 21:19)

Peter had crossed over and Jesus had removed his blind spot. After a three-year education, Peter was now ready to assume control.

Peter became the group's leader. He was the one to remind the apostles and disciples that to truly follow God they must forgo the ways of the world. He was the one who would decide all debates, not on what the world wanted, but what God wanted.

Why Peter? The Gospels tell us that Peter had consistently failed Jesus. When Jesus tried to teach him that he would walk on water, Peter fell into the water. When Jesus told the apostles that they would all abandon him during the darkness of the Passion, Peter boasted, "Though all become deserters because of you, I will never desert you."

Jesus told him, *"Truly I tell you, this very night, before the cock crows, you will deny me three times."* (Matthew 26:34) And indeed, Peter ended up denying he knew Jesus three times on the night of the crucifixion.

Early in his mission, Jesus rebuked Peter: *"Get behind me, Satan! You are a stumbling block to me; for you are setting your mind not on divine things but on human things."* (Matthew 16:23) Even after Jesus was crucified, Peter, like the others, slunk away to hide and returned to his former profession of fishing the Sea of Galilee.

Jesus had earlier said to Peter, *"And I tell you, you are Peter and on this rock I will build my church, and the gates of Hades will not prevail against it."* (Matthew 16:18) Peter was Jesus's designee, despite his failures. Jesus never gave up on Peter.

Peter, whose name in Greek means "rock," was seldom in doubt, though not always right. But Jesus saw another side of Peter. Jesus knew he was bold, he spoke up. He asked the tough questions of Jesus. He wasn't afraid of being wrong, he listened in order to learn. He was their change agent, the person the church would be built upon. Burdened by a lifetime of worldly influence, Peter finally forced himself to understand Jesus, and gave up his blind spot of not being totally committed.

At last, Peter fully understood that to be a leader for Jesus he had to sacrifice his personal desires, and he became what Jesus had seen buried inside him. Jesus had known Peter would fulfill his mission and do his job.

For forty days after Jesus rose, he stayed to help the Apostles and Peter, their new leader. On the fortieth day, now called the day of the Pentecost, Jesus ascended and the Holy Spirit descended on the apostles. On that very day, Peter delivered his first solo sermon, which brought three thousand people to The Way.

Later, Peter helped Paul solve the problem of converting the Gentiles. Many in Jerusalem knew of Paul and were afraid he was trying to trick them through a ruse. Peter prevailed by working the crowd and approving Paul's mission to make Christianity international.

Peter lived for some thirty years more. Through miracles and healing, he continued to build the base for The Way and became its rock. He was finally jailed and sentenced to be crucified. In one final homage to Jesus and testament to his sense of unworthiness by comparison, legend suggests that Peter asked to be crucified upside down. His wish was granted.

This bold, often arrogant man with numerous worldly blind spots became an obedient leader. Through tapping into Peter's heart and removing those blind spots, Jesus found a man who got get things done, was a great change agent, and listened to learn.

Two other apostles stand out as fine selections by Jesus who also had blind spots. The brothers James and John, like Peter, were fishermen from the Sea of Galilee, likely wealthier than the other apostles. Jesus called them "Sons of Thunder." If anything, they were too bold, for they could irritate the others, and they had their own blind spots: They were too quick to anger and too willing to bask in the spotlight.

At one point, after recognizing Jesus's power, their mother, Salome, the original "helicopter parent," approached Jesus with her sons. Kneeling, she asked if her sons could sit on his right and left hand in heaven, a remarkable request of God. Jesus simply replied, ***"You will indeed drink my cup, but to sit at my right hand and at my left, this is not mine to grant, but is for those for whom it has been prepared by my Father."*** (Matthew 20:23) Jesus didn't direct this answer to Salome, but to her sons. Bold men, they focused on their mission and not God's. Jesus selected them because they liked action and getting things done. They only needed to be tempered, a task for Jesus.

Once, when the band was traveling through Samaria looking for a place to rest, they were denied at the first house that looked inviting, largely because of a centuries-long feud between the Samaritans and the Jews. John asked Jesus to destroy the village in revenge. Jesus refused. Although he liked the brothers' passion, boldness, and zeal, he wasn't going to destroy a village to appease John.

After the Pentecost, the band carried on the mission as Peter had been doing. They all preached, they all healed, they all comforted, they all taught the Way of Jesus. In AD 44, James became the first of the apostles to be crucified by King Herod.

John was the last survivor of the original group. Two of the books of the Bible are attributed to him, either as sole author or as an influence. Tradition and some historical evidence supports his authorship of the Gospel of John, though later historians dispute this attribution. However, all agree that it is Johannine literature; John at a minimum had great influence on it.

The Gospel of John shows a softening and maturing of John that Jesus knew would come. John matured from the days he suggested burning a village in Samaria to being a man in God's thrall. We are no longer presented with an overly ambitious apostle; instead we see expressions of love. The word "love" is used in this Gospel twenty-eight times, almost as many as the other three Gospels combined. John had softened, but his passion was just as strong. He was still bold, but his zeal had been tempered. He quotes Jesus: *"I am giving you these commands so that you may love one another."* (John 15:17)

John's ministry survived a long time, and he himself developed a following. He moved from being an impetuous soul to being a guiding figure of the movement and lived into the late first century. Later historians would refer to John and James as "the Apostles of Love." Time tempered their impulsiveness.

John left us a message about teamwork by quoting Jesus: *"**What is born of the flesh is flesh and what is born of the Spirit is spirit.**"* (John 3:6) Here we find the basic principle of giving up our fleshly desires to join a common cause for good.

Jesus knew the brothers' passion would transform them into warm and assertive followers. Jesus knew their blind spots and knew time would temper these weaknesses. But Jesus also knew their strengths and maximized their gifts.

✜ ✜ ✜

Each year in my career, we had a company-wide employee review. The process required a tremendous amount of input from managers; sometimes the data would take months to sort through. People were graded and assigned to categories that ranged from "superior" to "failing." The review results, which we had to give to our employees, were overly complicated and ran to several pages.

I disagreed with this method, and searched for a simpler way. Many who worked for me would go home that evening to share the results with their loved ones. How could their family help or praise the employee with this excessive detail? How could the employee change or get better with so much to wade through? I began to wonder if the assessments were too much to relay all at once. The reviews included a significant amount of minutiae that clouded over the important facets. If I could distill the review to three to five important points covering strengths and blind spots before handing it over, I believed this winnowing would help my employees. By sticking to the main issues, I could help them make bigger strides forward.

What I noticed in the minutiae was that it all congealed into three to five points. In effect, if I relayed just those few points, I could address all the issues and the employee would have a workable assessment.

When we give our employees too much to work with, they become twisted up or ignore the review.

I didn't think of it at the time, but wasn't this really Jesus's approach? Jesus didn't focus on the minutiae with Matthew, Peter, James, and John, but on what would materially change them. Data wasn't important to Jesus. He looked for where their hearts were aligned and focused on the bigger issues to change their hearts.

Jesus didn't concentrate on résumés, he focused on the individuals themselves. Not on what they had done, but what they could do in the future. Many times when I would sit in sessions where we were deciding who would get promoted, the issue of age would come up, in effect short-circuiting the discussion of whether or not this was the best individual for the future. I would hear, "They are too old." Or I would hear, "They are too young." While somewhat relevant, this basic information had little to do with future performance or a person's spirit.

One of my employees at Foot Locker was a woman named Giovanna Cipriano. She was young, eager, and very passionate; sometimes I couldn't figure out if I was talking with a bright, well-educated potential executive or a foul-mouthed truck driver. Some would have objected to her language, but I saw it as a passionate effort to get things right. There was plenty wrong when we began to work together. She had endured difficult bosses, self-interested executives, and a failing company. I saw her outspokenness as an expression of frustration, because I knew what prompted the frustration, but I also knew that Giovanna had an extraordinarily high standard of excellence. She was bold, knew her craft, and worked harder than most to reach it.

When she talked to attorneys, many of whom were her seniors, she often knew more than they did. She was nearly faultless in preparing documents for the SEC. She sniffed out problems and provided solutions that were almost always right, well ahead of her peers.

She soon became our go-to person for accounting matters. If someone approached me with a solution to an accounting problem, my immediate question was "Have you talked to Giovanna?" If Giovanna said no, we would switch to another way. If she said yes, we moved forward.

The passions of her youth stayed with her. Being young didn't interfere with her spirit, which was directed to arriving at the right answer, not the expedient one. When we had an opening for chief accounting officer. Bob McHugh, her boss, and I immediately thought of Giovanna. The folks in Human Resources thought otherwise. They complained that she was too young; sure she was smart, but she didn't have the experience. We knew differently, and after a lengthy discussion I finally got the Human Resource executive to relent, and when Giovanna was only twenty-eight she became our chief accounting officer, an incredible achievement at a multibillion-dollar corporation. She was smart, devoted, and morally impeccable.

Later, Giovanna received praise from outside the company as well. The SEC and the ruling accounting boards would frequently cite our accounting as an example for other companies. In fact, our annual report was credited with having the best "Management, Discussion, and Analysis" section among the thousands that were filed in 2000. Accounting may be boring to some, but for a young executive, the plaudits were verification that doing your job with excellence and a strong spirit had paid off. Giovanna got great things done because she wasn't held back.

Over the years I promoted young and old based on their spirit. And Giovanna was bold, spirited, and smart. How people can help in the future is the most important determinant of who to assign or promote to a job. Future performance is indicated by a person's spirit and a commitment to the five criteria that make a great employee and teammate, not age.

✝ ✝ ✝

All of us, religious or not, if we are in sound mind, follow the Spirit. We feel guilty when we hurt a neighbor or a friend. We want to make sure we do good. We seek the right answer, not just the one that satisfies our ambitions. We often ignore our personal interests to follow the right way.

When we want to satisfy our flesh, we are being led by our flesh. When we live with the Spirit, our actions are to satisfy God—or good. Almost every hour we confront this conflict: flesh or spirit. Flesh, invariably self-directed, is filled with peril. Spirit, which will not satisfy flesh, requires sacrifice. The Spirit is always directed away from ourselves to God and our friends and neighbors. We choose how we lead our lives. Like Jesus, we are fulfilled when we hire for our teams those with the Spirit.

Jesus built his team with people of promise, those who were bold and whose goal was to do good. He looked in unusual places and found unusual people—a despised tax collector, fishermen, people from the marketplace who wanted to rise higher. Jesus's job was to bring out the assets that he saw hidden within them to be harvested. They listened, they solved problems, they loved their neighbors and warmly but assertively got things done.

CHAPTER 11

JESUS, MARKETPLACE COACH

"I am the way, and the truth, and the life."

–JOHN 14:6

"*I am the way, and the truth, and the life.*" This is a hallmark Christian thought; it implies that through Jesus we experience God's values in our personal lives and in the marketplace. The statement *"I am the way"* represents many aspects of Jesus: Jesus as God's intermediary, the model of sacrifice, a way of loving God and our neighbor, a way of unwinding the ethical dilemmas facing us in the marketplace—a way of living life.

Who is Jesus to our current marketplace? He is a bestselling author. He is the founder of the largest organization in the world. He worked his way up from the bottom in the marketplace. If he booked a speaking tour in contemporary times, he would sell out every venue on the tour. He is a gifted strategist and keeps the road straight. He has been there and knows our issues. But most importantly his words and presence are as available to us today as they were for the first-century marketplace.

How do we get on Jesus's schedule for a session of life coaching? How do we develop a relationship with Jesus that becomes intimate and helpful? How do we tap into his way as a guide to help us with our customers and colleagues? Simple. Read the Bible, and specifically the Sermon on the Mount (Matthew 5–7), and develop a personal relationship with Jesus through prayer. Jesus will be there. Remarkably, Jesus is present today in both his teachings and through prayer.

Many people that have this successful coaching arrangement start with prayer to smooth out their weaknesses. Prayer that asks for Jesus's help. Prayer that is continuous and reciprocal. Many start their day with prayer as a way of consulting with Jesus, sharing their dreams and problems. They acknowledge they know Jesus's power and purpose. They petition for a solution and respectfully praise him.

Over time they have answers given to them in different circumstances, through reading the Bible and through other means. They learn to read the clues that are intimately tied to prayer life. They see changes in their heart. They notice unusual things smoothing out their lives. Over time they have created with Jesus a connected life.

Through this relationship Jesus as a marketplace coach will challenge and test the way we think. We will be given goals to achieve that will put us in opposition to our old way of life. We will have to choose which path we take, many times moving from short-term gains to long-term solutions. We will be tested, and when we succeed we will know it was Jesus who helped and encouraged us. When we fail, we always get a second chance. We will receive grace.

Jesus will send us down paths to unusual places we never expected, sometimes to challenging places we don't think we can survive. He will always be with us, whether we succeed or fail. Jesus knows the way.

Over time, when we meet with Jesus daily, he becomes a habit. He seeps into our thoughts. We listen and respond. We talk and Jesus hears. We observe and we see. It starts slowly and over time takes over our being. Daily prayer is available to all of us.

Hidden away in the Gospel of Matthew is a road map to help us know what Jesus wants from us. He spells out a revelation of God that shows us how to exist. When we connect the Sermon on the Mount to a life of daily prayer, we create our own roadmap with Jesus, one that illustrates our desired values and God's values. It is a detailed game plan for marketplace workers and leaders from "the greatest coach of all time."

Jesus provides this road map to us through the Sermon on the Mount, which appears in the Gospel of Matthew in its entirety from chapters five through seven. In it is found the words of life. The first full sermon by Jesus, it expands the Ten Commandments from a list of laws into something we follow through our hearts. A way of living. If followed perfectly, this way will allow us to thrive and live a purposeful life. The Sermon on the Mount contains the revelation from God for how to live. A revelation that moves us from our natural selves to a life connected with the spirit that is God.

In addition to an expansion and lengthy discourse on the value of the Ten Commandments, we find in the sermon the Golden Rule, the Beatitudes, the Lord's Prayer, and lessons like "turning the other cheek." A short read, maybe fifteen minutes at the most, reveals everything. The sermon becomes a place to go when we are unsettled. A place to soothe our anger, rid ourselves of greed, and open our hearts. A place where when we begin, we can't ignore what we read. A place that makes us examine ourselves. Honestly and simply written, the Sermon on the Mount reveals all.

In setting the scene for the longest discourse by Jesus in the Bible, we need to consider that Jesus had traveled throughout Galilee performing miracles, healing and talking with those of the region. He had been baptized by John the Baptist, tested by Satan, and gathered up his apostles as he prepared to begin his three-year mission for God. It was after these events that Jesus delivered this thesis on life and the values of God.

Jesus found a mountainside that would accommodate the throngs gathered to hear him. As he delivered his inaugural address, great crowds swarmed beneath the mount, drawn by his reputation. He began this most famous of all teaching moments by describing the character of people desired by God, one that would lead to being blessed and to a fulfilling life of purpose. He spoke of a character that would lead to thriving and not just surviving. He presented a radically different set of ideals; those focused on love and humility called the Beatitudes. In them lie the essence of the character and attitude in our hearts that God desires.

Jesus laid them out by saying the following:

"Blessed are the poor in spirit: for theirs is the kingdom of heaven. (Matthew 5:3)

Blessed are those who mourn: for they will be comforted. (5:4)

Blessed are the meek: for they will inherit the earth. (5:5)

Blessed are those who hunger and thirst for righteousness, for they will be filled. (5:6)

Blessed are the merciful, for they will be shown mercy. (5:7)

Blessed are the pure in heart, for they will see God. (5:8)

Blessed are the peacemakers, for they will be called children of God. (5:9)

Blessed are those who are persecuted for righteousness' sake, for theirs is the kingdom of heaven. (5:10)

Blessed are you when people revile you and persecute you and utter all kinds of evil against you falsely on my account. Rejoice and be glad, for your reward in heaven is great, for in the same way they persecuted the prophets who were before you." (5:11–12)

When taken together the Beatitudes express a combined sense of humility, compassion, and spirituality. They provide a sense of our own behavior in approaching life, our customers, and the marketplace. When we are wronged, we are not to change our character. We are to maintain purity and search for the right way. We are called to find peaceful solutions and not use gasoline to put out a fire. We are to show mercy and provide comfort. For many of this period, this was a remarkable change in perspective. Many from the marketplace were just surviving and spent a large part of their day defending against or reacting to wrongs. They were forced by the religious elite to be strictly obedient to a stifling set of rules and traditions. Jesus took these laws and traditions and supplemented the Ten Commandments with a discourse for the heart. This isn't a matter of "an eye for an eye and a tooth for a tooth." It's about "turning the other cheek," not getting caught up with reacting to others but reacting to the ways of God.

It is also about who are we trying to impress and for what purpose. Later in the sermon, Jesus said, *"Beware of practicing your piety before others in order to be seen by them; for then you have no reward from your Father in heaven."* (Matthew 6:1) Many of the scribes and Pharisees, trapped by a judgmental heart and power, would commonly make sure that their prayers and donations were seen by the community. They wanted to show all how great they were. Their prayer shawls hung very long and they created tortuous traditions for the masses to comply with. All in an attempt to prove their piety. Jesus reminds us that our acts of mercy, charity, and prayer are not to impress others but to let God know privately that our hearts are aligned with his.

Jesus then took on the prevailing, overly legalistic views of the Ten Commandments, those ten facets of life that were given to Moses on two stone tablets. For centuries, they had been the guidepost for the people of Israel. While Jesus was very supportive of the Commandments, his disagreement with the religious elite was on how to live in accordance with them, not to live as slaves to the laws in order to prove how good we are, but to follow them in the deepest parts of our hearts, with a deeply connected commitment to God and our neighbor.

In the Gospels Jesus is seen frequently arguing with the Pharisees, sometimes referred to by him as hypocrites. He also had an issue with the Pharisees as far as their understanding of the Commandments; they did not live what they taught. They promulgated false authority and false teaching. They were trapped and lured in by their power, which led them astray through its temptations.

To be clear, Jesus and Pharisees and other religious elites didn't disagree on the fact that the Commandments were the revelation of the Word of God. They differed on the approach. Jesus revealed that the basis of the Commandments was love, "love for God and love for our neighbor." Through of hearts we connect with God. The Pharisees and other religious elites saw the Commandments as a "to do" list, not something felt, but an exact listing of God's will.

For example, the sixth commandment states, "You shall not murder." On a technical and exact basis, its meaning is obvious. But Jesus saw this and more. He points this out by saying, ***"You have heard it said to those of ancient times, 'You shall not murder'; and 'whoever murders shall be liable for judgement.' But I say to you that if you are angry with a brother or sister, you will be liable to judgment..."***

(Matthew 5:22) Jesus extended the meaning beyond the physical act of ending a person's life to being angry with a person. He made it clear that to comply with the sixth commandment doesn't mean following just a literal interpretation, but an interpretation using an attitude of nonjudgmental love. While we can be upset by situations, we should have no anger in our hearts toward others, regardless of their actions. Those of us in the marketplace, regardless of how we are treated, are to maintain a posture of fair play and maintain a heart that is pointed to doing the right thing.

✝ ✝ ✝

At Foot Locker, at times we had to sell many small and unnecessary businesses. In one particular case we had to sell some real estate that wasn't important to our future but would raise much needed cash. After a rather simple negotiation with a buyer, we established a price and closing date. Initially, the buyer wanted a protracted schedule and we wanted an earlier date. We agreed to meet in the middle and signed our agreement. We inspected the properties and made them suitable for the sale. I remember reminding our facility team that we should do all we could to make the properties perfect for the sale.

About a month before the closing date, our attorneys approached me and told me that the buyer wanted to renegotiate the signed agreement to the buyer's original time frame. Generally, if either the buyer or seller wants to renegotiate, it is appropriate to offer compensation in some form to the party being inconvenienced. In this case there was no offer to compensate Foot Locker for the delay in closing. I told our attorneys to say no and remind the buyer that the date was previously negotiated. Expecting no further word, we moved ahead on our end.

However, a week before closing, when all the preparations were well under way, when we had talked with our banks and they were happy, our attorneys came into my office and appeared grim. "The buyer is moving the closing date back," I was told.

Angrily, I replied "no way."

Our attorneys explained that technically the buyer could do this, by using the "cure period." In other words, if he failed to show up at the closing, he had ten business days to resolve his default. This ten-day period is called the "cure period." The buyer told us that this was what he was going to do and to be prepared. In the marketplace this is a very unusual and underhanded act, but legally correct.

My first response was anger. The buyer was taking advantage of my company, an unbelievable insult. I called the head of facilities, Peter Cupps, who was in charge of preparing the property, and told him to only broom clean the building per the contract and not go the extra mile. But Peter Cupps said, "Boss you told us to make it perfect."

"I know I did," I replied.

After about ten minutes of calming me down, Peter told me, "It doesn't matter how he behaves, it matters how we behave."

I knew that Peter was right, but I was stung by being taken advantage of.

We sold the property and delivered it in the best condition we could. My anger was more of personal pride than intellect. Thankfully, Peter took the stand of ignoring our being abused and focused on Foot Locker's value of delivering a quality product. While the buyer complied with the strictest interpretations of the agreement, he failed to live up to the spirit of it. Thankfully, Peter stayed in the spirit. By taking the high road, Peter maintained our value of doing the right thing, regardless of how we were treated. Our work was always to be completed to its highest levels regardless of circumstance. Our employees would see Peter's leadership as a reinforcement of that value. Peter was right in what he did and with the alignment of his heart.

In the Sermon on the Mount, Jesus created the Golden Rule by saying, ***"In everything do to others as you would have them do to you; for this is the law and the prophets."*** (Matthew 7:12) This verse contains two important points. Jesus asks us to remember how we want to be treated, and that in this way we should treat others. He wants us to love our neighbor as we love ourselves. He implores us from the marketplace to sell and make products that we personally would want to buy. He is asking us to always ensure in our business practices that we consider the customer and not make extra profits at the customer's expense. Here we go back to Leonard Bean's original philosophy for L.L.Bean, "Sell good merchandise at a reasonable profit, treat your customers like human beings and they will always come back for more." This motto still exists today, in writing, for L.L.Bean.

When you call L.L.Bean's customer service line, they almost always answer the phone within a few rings and with a human voice. There are no computers that ask you to go through a number of steps before you can get a live person. Just a human voice ready to help.

In retail there is a saying that has existed for centuries, "The customer is always right." At first this seems like a caving in to the wish of every customer. Corporations sometimes remember the one-off customer who has taken advantage of their policies, and some retailers have collapsed their treatment of customer service into a bunker mentality because of these isolated abuses. They create policies designed to protect themselves from the infrequent customer who takes advantage of them. And in turn they restrict their loyal customers' access to exceptional customer service. In situations like this, rules set in and our good customers find it hard to do business with us. Our hearts become hardened to all our customers. Over time the loyal customers silently leave and our business suffers, all so we can be protected from the infrequent customer who abuses us.

✟ ✟ ✟

Jesus was also very specific about our life goals in this sermon. In Matthew 6:24 he reorients the goals of the marketplace, by saying, *"No one can serve two masters; for a slave will either hate the one and love the other, or be devoted to one and despise the other. You cannot serve God and wealth."*

Remember that we can often substitute the word "employee" for what the word "slave" meant in that time. In this verse Jesus is only reorienting our view of why we make a living. If our pursuit is exclusively to amass a great fortune without regard to God, our families, and our neighbor, then we are on a dead-end street. Our net worth becomes more important than our self-worth. This call is a warning and good advice.

Over time, when we pursue wealth we become disoriented and relax our personal set of ethics. We begin saying, *Just one more time.* We begin a justification process of rationalizing why we are making the morally suspect choices we are making at work. Slowly, temptation overtakes us, and years later we find ourselves in a spiritual spot we never wanted to be in.

There are stories littering our daily headlines today that expose the risk of chasing money and the expansion of our net worth, Bernie Madoff being a prime example. Bernie's descent started slowly, driven by a need for big houses and a fancy lifestyle similar to his peers'. He liked the life of private jets and lavish vacations he saw that others had. He got sucked in and lowered his ethics. As the former non-executive chairman of the NASDAQ stock exchange, he was exposed to the great wealth others were accumulating. He wanted his piece of this pie. He started his firm in 1960. At first he ran a legitimate business helping people with investing their money. Over time, he began to stretch out and promise higher and more consistent returns than his peers. In turn more money flowed his way. He began to cut corners. He became riveted on generating more income for himself to establish a lifestyle of excess. His standards for following the rules had become lax.

By the 1990s his Ponzi scheme was in full gear. He would ask people to invest with him and promised extraordinarily consistent high returns. To accomplish this, he concealed and doctored his reports. While he paid out these returns as promised to some, he used investor monies for himself. Everything worked well. His clients got their paper returns and he siphoned off money to pay for his extraordinary lifestyle. As long as the stock market grew, he could cover up his abuse of his customers' money.

By 2008 his firm had grown to be considered the top "market maker" business on Wall Street. He was riding high. Then in 2008, the Great Recession hit, and the house of cards came tumbling down. Stocks became devalued by as much as forty percent, in effect exposing Bernie's crime. Warren Buffett has a great saying about shoddy business practices: "When the tide goes out, it exposes those who are swimming naked." Bernie was swimming naked!

Sixty-five billion dollars was missing. The largest such scam in history. The money had been wasted on Madoff's lifestyle. Madoff pled guilty to many counts of fraud and is currently in jail.

In the aftermath, billions in life savings were revealed to have been lost by innocent investors. Madoff's son, who worked for him, committed suicide. His wife struggles day to day. Madoff's sentence was one hundred fifty years in jail. All to have a house with a pool in Miami, like those he admired.

Imagine if his master was God, and we could rewind the clock. This astute financial man would have been successful, his son would still be alive, his clients would have their retirement funds, and his wife would have a husband and a life.

Jesus talks about this process of descending into darkness in 6:22–23 of Matthew by saying, *"The eye is the lamp of the body. So if your eye is healthy, your whole body will be full of light; but if your eye is unhealthy, your whole body will be full of darkness. If then the light in you is darkness, how great is the darkness!"*

Jesus was also aware that having an attitude of love to God and neighbor would expose you to risk. He provides a solution to avoid be taken advantage of in verse 7:6 of Matthew. He says, *"Do not give what is holy to dogs; and do not throw your pearls before swine, or they will trample them under foot and turn and maul you."*

Jesus knew that there were those who seek to gain from others and that people with pure hearts would be exposed to these wolves. He asked us to be shrewd in our discernment to avoid being taken advantage of by these people.

I have an acquaintance who calls me here and there. In each call he is looking for a favor. Knowing my deep contact list, he frequently asks me to put in a good word for him or to solicit information from my contacts. To ask for this kind of information and then pass it on to my acquaintance would be at best duplicitous and at worst illegal. In one case he asked me to contact the CEO of rue21, whom I knew well from my time serving on their board of directors, a request that could significantly hurt my relationship with the CEO. I gently refused, in spite of the potential short-term gain for myself. A few months later the CEO of rue21 called asking for me to provide him some assistance. I was glad I could help and glad I hadn't complied with my acquaintance's request.

Over the years, I have noticed he never asks how I am doing or about my family. He doesn't call to find out about my golf game, in spite of my always asking him about his life. I am no more than an apple from an apple tree to my acquaintance, someone who can be picked to help his life. He is a potentially dangerous wolf.

I usually try to politely avoid agreeing or to ignore his request. Over time, as I have become less valuable to him, his calls have diminished. It is these people Jesus cautions us about.

✝ ✝ ✝

Jesus also stresses the importance of prayer. Prayer is our own personal daily dialogue with God. As people from my old marketplace have gotten to know my current life's direction, they have asked how to pray. Even those of great faith ask. Prayer is deeply personal and is a continuing dialogue for those committed to a life with God.

Prayer contains four important ingredients. The first is praise and recognition of God. The second is petition, and the third is thanksgiving. And lastly, the fourth is a recognition of Jesus as our savior intermediary.

In the Sermon on the Mount Jesus gives us the model for this type of prayer by saying, *"Our Father in heaven, hallowed be your name. Your kingdom come. Your will be done, on earth as it is in heaven. Give us this day our daily bread. And forgive us our debts, as we also have forgiven our debtors. And do not bring us to the time of trial, but rescue us from the evil one."* (Matthew 6:9–13) Over time, this prayer, commonly called the Lord's Prayer, has been modified to reflect contemporary language, but these are the actual words spoken by Jesus.

For those wanting to pray, this prayer contains the four steps. I often use it as a part of my daily routine, and to avoid being robotic I will substitute phrases. For instance, it says, "Give us this day our daily bread." If I have an important meeting that day, I will add in "Give me your guidance and strength to help me with wisdom for my meeting." Or "Please provide me with the recognition of your will."

There are many who pray with extraordinary ease and make the words sing. They are inspirational people and they bring God closer to us. However, in the early morning when we are alone with God, they are not with us. Jesus has provided a prayer template for us, one we can expand upon and trust.

As we start to pray, our conversations with God begin to last throughout the day and we begin to connect our lives to God's response to prayer. Some will say these responses are mere coincidences, but over time the validity of the responses diminishes this doubt.

A client of mine, whom we will call John, found himself unemployed. In spite of strong credentials and connections, he was stymied in his attempts to find work. Many potential employers were concerned about the way he presented himself. He was overly wordy and many times would drone on without giving the potential employer time to talk. When he contacted me, he was beaten up. He had heard I could help.

I was frank with him: He had two things working against him. The first was that he was unemployed, which always makes potential employers suspicious, a suspicion he couldn't correct unless he tried harder than others. The second, in his zeal to express himself he was too wordy. That we could correct. For months we worked every week on networking and applying for jobs. We worked on ingenious ways to make contacts. We worked on his interviewing skills. Most importantly we worked on prayer and making him "humble, precise, and concise."

Many weeks when we started our sessions, I found John in despair. He was lonely and felt rejected. It was causing him to doubt his value. He would sink into an abyss of worthlessness. Many times we worked first on his self-worth. We prayed, and he even went away on a retreat to determine what God wanted from him. No answers were coming. He kept marching on with his cycle. Despair to hope and back again.

This process of moving from lamentation to self-determination is very common with my clients. Failure and lack of hope produce a need for lamentation. Then a glimmer of success encourages them to continue to move forward. This process repeats itself at times for all of us until we are finally aware of Jesus's presence. We only discover his presence through prayer connected with circumstance. We are crest-fallen when no help is apparent and encouraged when we begin to get answers, and so it goes, back and forth. But Jesus as God works mysteriously and circumstantially. He works on his own schedule not ours, but he always remembers our lament.

In working with John, this point was discussed many times, but for the individual in distress it is hard to sit quietly. Many times that person is alone with his or her own thoughts and has to fight the despair through the darkest of moments. Prayer, patience, and faith are the only cures for those quiet moments of despair.

John worked hard on reducing his input in interviews and learned to listen first. Afterward we would review the results and discuss what he could do differently. Prayer became his form of lamentation, and changing his method of communication became his self-determination. Overtime he began to connect the two. He began to have more success and was able to get past the first interview and on to the final interview.

Finally, in a quiet moment, he got the call. He was hired. He was an employee! He was of value. God had answered his prayers. His moments of feeling forlorn became memories. Without a blasting siren or a showering of confetti Jesus answered him. He was of value.

When John started his new job, he quickly discovered that a fraud had been committed. *Great*, he said sarcastically to himself. Wondering what to do wasn't the problem. He knew he had to tell the CEO and the board of directors. His problem was he was afraid he was going to be fired. He was fearful of his future and dreaded going back to that horrible place he had been.

Again we worked on prayer to build up his personal strength. He prepared all the facts. The night before he delivered the news, he didn't sleep. The next morning, he had his meetings. Each person he talked to thanked him and showed appreciation. At his meeting with the CEO, after thanking him, the CEO commented, "I really appreciate your jumping right in and getting involved. We made a good hire."

John left work early that day. He drove the fifty minutes home and felt a slow washing of relief. As the drive wore on, his pain was replaced with gratitude. As he entered his apartment, he sat in his favorite chair and quietly thanked God.

John and I talked the following day. I expressed my pride in his journey. John thanked me for all my help. I reminded him that it wasn't me, it was a lifetime of being surrounded by great people and the power of Jesus. It was his prayers and resolute doggedness to thrive in an unfriendly place.

He asked me if I had time to take on another client. I told him I could and I had an opening on Wednesdays at five. John's time every week. He passed on his friend's name and contact information, and I reminded him to call anytime. But he had completed this journey.

Jesus didn't answer John's prayer with a thunderous voice or a "star spangled" salute. Jesus answered John with a quiet and unexpected solution, one that involved many twists and turns, but one in which it became very obvious that what appeared to be dangerous and substandard was actually good.

He continued to thank me, and in a final gesture, I reminded him of the Sermon on the Mount and that it contains all the life guidance he needed. In fifteen minutes of quiet and slow reading of Matthew 5 to 7, he would find the comfort and insight of Jesus.

✝ ✝ ✝

Jesus ended his sermon by explaining and summarizing why these words of life are important. He said, *"Everyone then who hears these words of mine and acts on them will be like a wise man who built his house on rock. The rain fell, the floods came, and the winds blew and beat on that house, but it did not fall, because it had been founded on rock. And everyone who hears these words of mine and does not act on them will be like a foolish man who built his house on sand. The rain fell, and the floods came, and the winds blew and beat against that house, and it fell—and great was its fall!"* (Matthew 7:24–27)

In fifteen quiet minutes, we can receive the advice of the coach who is the *"greatest of all time."* A short read that allows us to become centered before we head off to earn a living. A short read when we need an answer: Jesus is the way, and the truth, and the life.

EPILOGUE

"For surely I know the plans I have for you, says the LORD, plans for your welfare and not for harm, to give you a future with hope."

–JEREMIAH 29:11

It is now the late afternoon of my life, nearing dusk. I approach every day with the same passion that existed in me when I was twenty. It has been a long walk from that quiet morning in the spring of 2009 as I've transitioned away from an old life to a new one. It's been a transition from living by impulse to trying to live with the spirit of God, and life feels new. Sometimes I am tempted to go back to the place I came from, but I know I don't belong there. I belong here.

Over the last few years I have changed my "to do" list, and it now comes from God. Today my life consists mostly of helping inner city youth get access to elite colleges or guiding those who are helping in recovery from disasters. I spend my days assisting others in getting jobs and helping businesses and people become solvent. I am a servant. I've tried to get back into the business world, but it no longer works for me.

The marketplace, though, is still important to me. I follow *The Wall Street Journal*, and I have my stocks and other investments.

Connie and I have a financial plan to serve us for the rest of our lives. At this point in my life, I'm third in my list of priorities: God, family, me. When I say "God," I include his Son and the Holy Spirit. "Family" comprises not only Connie and my daughters, but my neighbors and friends. As for me: Well, I'm the fellow who wrote this book, but by many measures, you're more important than I am, since I am but a servant.

I have traveled to places in the world to help others, including a trip to Africa to help orphans recover from losing their parents to AIDS. I completed a master's degree in Divinity and in May 2018, hopefully, I will receive a doctorate degree in Ministry. I have started a business called Gideon Partners. And every day I talk to God. I am still not perfect, still prone to let surface my natural self and with it anger and selfishness. Jesus has been chiseling for a lifetime; it is only recently, since my early morning walk, that I have connected Jesus and his values with my life.

Calling my new business Gideon Partners makes it very personal. Gideon was a man from the ancient marketplace, whom God called to leave his work and work for him. A modest man who resisted God. He doubted the value of God, and along his journey he continued to be forced to follow God's ways. He would throw up road blocks to God and lacked the faith that following God would be the best way. Eventually God won him over, and Gideon went on to help save the Israelites, God's people.

One incident of extreme stress from the past showed me God was always with me but I wasn't fully bought in. Only later in life did I realize that I had been guided by a higher power. It was that critical moment in Foot Locker's history that saved them from ruin.

In the summer of 1999, I was in a meeting with Roger Farah. My basic principle as a CFO was that I was like a defensive football coach. I didn't care if the ball was on the half-inch line, you cannot let the other team score. If it's anything else, you're not playing with the right heart, and you must play with the right intent.

"We're going to file for bankruptcy," Roger told me.

I was stunned. "You want to file a bankruptcy. I don't agree with that." The ball was on the half-yard line; they hadn't scored yet. "Look, I did the research. Few retailers have emerged from bankruptcy. If we file, it's like giving up." To Roger's credit, and similar to other conversations, he agreed and we continued our goal line stand. This conversation changed everything for Foot Locker. It meant not giving up in spite of overwhelming physical evidence that it was time. It meant trusting in the power of those working to save Foot Locker to continue trying. I didn't know it at the time, but if we tried the right way, God's way, we would survive.

Later, during personal reflection, I really felt that I was guided in that meeting, that I was listening to Jesus. He was asking me to do something difficult. To do anything else is to give away your treasure, lessen your self-worth. Giving in was the wrong answer. We fought to survive and won.

At Gideon Partners, I approach all my clients with the same attitude: never give up and always search for the way of Jesus. Jesus's way isn't always easy. Miracles and success involve hard work. Problems don't get resolved by winning the lottery, but by a combined walk with Jesus that takes us through valleys of darkness. These are the times when we are uniquely alone. But we are always with Jesus.

The work of Gideon Partners involves a functional step-by-step process. It all starts with asking what Jesus's goals for us are. To discover this important life information, we connect with Jesus through prayer and watch for circumstances. Sometimes it takes moments of reflection and sometimes days of wrestling. Jesus invites us into a discussion. He stands knocking at our door. He wants to invite us to dine with him.

When we connect and discover our life's direction, we have to give something up. For me it was giving up working in the marketplace, and instead working for God *with* the marketplace. To do this required six years of study in Theology. During that study, I had to learn how to connect my past experiences with my new knowledge.

We don't give up our worldly desires easily. We fight back and we rationalize. We take steps in the wrong direction only to be rebuffed. Circumstances force us back to our new path. With this new direction we discover valleys as we navigate through our new world. We experience regrets and in our darkest moments we desire to turn back, moving away from God's new direction. Initially, as we begin this journey we may find ourselves in constant crisis. We are in a furnace not to be destroyed but to be hardened for the task in front of us.

For me entering the world of academia and study was difficult. I was no longer the boss, but the one being instructed. I had to learn to write. In my undergraduate program, I failed English courses and had to make them up in the summer. I was strong at math and logic but extraordinarily weak in the most important skill of theological studies, writing. I barely passed the writing admissions requirement, but got accepted at Drew.

My first two-page paper took six hours to write. Luckily, I made friends with the librarian at Drew, Ernie Rubenstein, who painstakingly undertook the task of helping me learn to write. What took my classmates an hour to write took me many hours. Over time, I reached a level that was competent enough for me to write my papers. And thankfully, my logic and insights were strong enough to rise above my weakness. In 2013, I graduated with a 3.8 GPA and won the Daniel B. Kidder Award for highest GPA in Pastoral Theology.

I tried my hand at working in the church, but found it to be difficult and a source of great frustration. I wasn't satisfied. Another valley of discouragement. Three hard years to get my master's degree and I wasn't where God wanted me to be.

I set up my business, believing this was what God wanted from me. In the first year it was a huge commercial success. My monthly income from fees earned was forty to sixty thousand dollars a month. But at no point was I ever happy. I stayed troubled. I was impatient, and many of my old habits returned. In 2015 I flew over 100 times. I was not where I was supposed to be. I wasn't asked for my theological advice; I was wanted for my business advice. In 2016, I rearranged my mission and gave up providing help unless I could help from a Christian viewpoint.

I then started to get glimmers from my old world. People from my past would call me for theological advice. I would hear, "It's amazing how you can simplify and make Jesus so accessible." The stories I told of Jesus were no longer mysteries to these people from my past; they were spoken in a language they understood. I didn't use fancy words or overly complex doctrine but rather words and stories that brought Jesus alive.

It was these conversations that gave me purpose and thrilled me. It wasn't money, it was helping that gave me joy. Through these glimmers I crafted a new life that made me anxious for the morning to arrive. I went to sleep looking forward to the next day, to a life where things played out excitingly, on and on, as my life extended with Jesus always present.

Now I share my stories about Jesus and the wonderful people who have helped me in my life. I take my listeners and readers through a process to be liberated from those events in their lives that pin them down and bind them to just surviving. My goal is help them rise up, release their bonds, and thrive. But first they must give up what holds them down and give in to Jesus.

Part of this giving up means changing what holds us back. It starts with becoming external. Learning that through our giving we find our purpose. Learning that smiling brings us where we want to be. Learning that people are to be loved and helped. The stomach needs food and the heart needs people and a purpose.

When I do my employment counseling work, I give my clients a two-day exercise. From the start of the morning until they go to bed at night, they should try to make the day better, richer, more inspired for every person they meet.

When you go to Starbucks, compliment the person waiting on you. I tell my clients, "If you're in a meeting, praise ideas and listen." I ask them to hold doors for strangers and to wait for the other person and let them walk in front. Pay attention to other people, and if they need help with their groceries, help. Say hi to complete strangers when they are on their walks and make sure you are smiling every time you meet someone. In every action draw out of your heart a genuine interest. No fake "How are you," but a real external connection.

In this process I ask them to observe people's reactions and see if they can discover something in each person. We should challenge ourselves to see if we can discover something inside each person that we meet and if we can help. We never know when God needs us to help someone.

I was on a train to Washington recently and spent most of my time reading a book called *Experiencing God*, by Henry Blackaby. When I could, I acknowledged the conductor and smiled. Near the end of the trip I was standing in the vestibule waiting to depart and the conductor followed me out. She simply asked if I knew how to pray.

"I do. Why do you ask?"

"I'm struggling with God and you seem like someone that could help."

I told her about the Lord's Prayer and discussed its structure briefly with her. She thanked me and said it helped.

"You should try it daily and be sincere. Try to allow it to play out over time. God will answer," I said.

I am not sure I helped complete her journey; most likely I was just one of the many people she would meet on her personal path toward Jesus. But at that moment we connected.

One of my clients dubbed this process of actively trying to connect with people "extreme empathy." This process may sound trivial, and at first we may doubt its importance, and by the end of the day you're exhausted when you first try. But over time it becomes natural, and we start the movement from being internal to being external. We begin to become empathetic to others. We give others the space to affirm themselves to a complete stranger. We learn to pick up the clues of who they are. We become trusted. We move from "I" to "they." We learn that people like people who like them.

When my clients engage in this effort, the pattern is the same. At first it is awkward and forced, but over time they learn to read body language and the conversations smooth out. They reveal wonderful encounters with complete strangers. They have affirmed lives that needed to be affirmed. They become trusted and liked. And as we adopt this behavior of extreme empathy in our work lives, we become more engaged and people begin to seek us out. We create a spirit of partnership.

Another practice I help people with is how to interview. It starts with knowing what companies in the marketplace want. The marketplace wants partners who are serious, qualified, polite, courteous, and know how to be team players. If you go in for an interview and use the word "I" repeatedly in the first five minutes, the interview might go on, but it's over practically before it starts. We also know it from sports: "There is no 'I' in team," and that holds true in the marketplace also.

A client of mine kept getting interviews for jobs he was qualified for with a strong background. But he kept missing out, especially in the final round. I asked him to go back and see if he could get feedback as to why he wasn't chosen, then develop a list from each conversation. The assignment was to ask the recruiters not why he didn't get the job, but what he could have done better. This simple change, I said, would elicit more honest feedback. One thing came back from these conversations that gave him the clue. He was too arrogant and appeared to be too cocky. While highly qualified technically, he needed to become more external to those interviewing him and show interest in them and not just in proving how smart he was as a candidate. He said the word "I" too much.

A friend of mine, when asked why he was successful, said, "I learned that the marketplace is very accepting as long as you're not a jerk." A blunt statement that reveals a critical lesson about how we should conduct ourselves. Our credentials may be solid, but our approach is more important.

To bury our treasure and follow Jesus is compatible with a normal business life, whether you're a CEO or just starting out. When we follow Jesus, we embark on a journey that requires patience and practice, listening to the spirit and being guided. It's about serving where you can make a difference and looking for like-minded people. The rewards of the journey are palpable every day: joy, a clear conscience, moral behavior no matter what it costs. It is, in fact, a journey from "me" to a family to God.

We move from being internal focusers to loving our neighbor. This shows its value in employment interviews, sales calls, personal relationships, and daily conversations. By moving away from the self and into the hearts of others we become partners with humanity.

Gideon Partners is now growing, not commercially, but with lives that are changed. My wife always asks, "How do you find these clients?" I tell her I don't know, they just appear. They come through referrals and coincidence. They just appear. I am glad to help.

This is a significant change for my life. I was a corporate predator, prone to anger and self-importance. As time moved on in my career, I dug a deep hole of selfishness. I moved further away from the stirrings of my youth; I became my own God and asked others to serve. In a violent shake-up of my heart, I began the slow move back to being what God wanted me to be.

Life isn't stressful or tiring anymore. Each morning I wake up excited to live my day. It has been a long journey home. A journey with many valleys. Each valley scraped away more of the faults from the past. Each valley showed me a new way. The valleys are not the pleasant places of life, but they are important. The distant mountain-tops sometimes seemed too far away. I trudged forward, sometimes forced on my march by Jesus or sometimes through myself. Slowly I continued, happier than I was.

Finally, today, I know my direction and am moving, both in my mental state and physically, to a place I belong.

In early 2017, on the day we were moving from our family home. I got up very early in the morning to spend one last quiet moment in my house. We were leaving our home; a place that saw many mile-stones. Four daughters were raised here. In this home we raised two chinchillas, two rabbits, fish, and two dogs. Gone was our dog Buddy, who sat with me each morning as I learned to walk this new life. He was handsome, the George Clooney of dogs, a good friend who only wanted to help. It was his life's goal.

It was here in this house that my career had played out. Gone were the pencil marks that showed my daughters' growth and the pictures on the fridge that marked the life of a family. The trophies that marked my career had been packed away. This was a place where a life had played out. A place where I moved from being internal to being external. It was a bittersweet moment, marking a transition from old to new.

The girls were spread out throughout the world now, and we were proud of each one of them. In place of our family, a younger version would move in here. This is a home that raises families.

For a few moments longer, it was still our house. Connie and I are crossing over a great divide in the late afternoon of our lives, to a new life full of promise. It will be a life filled with Jesus. A life to be continued.

In Jesus's name we pray.

ACKNOWLEDGMENTS

I started this journey nearly two years ago. Inspired by friends, like Tom Locke, head of the Texas Methodist Foundation, Bishop John Schol, Bishop of the United Methodist Church, and many friends. All telling me I had a unique story to tell. A story about Jesus and the business world. A different story than previously told about our Lord and Savior, Jesus the Christ. A way to make the stories of Jesus more vivid for those who worked in the modern marketplace.

My goal in writing this book was to create a sustainable piece of literature that would endure. Knowing full well that my English skills were significantly lacking to accomplish this task, I sought help from those who were superior in their abilities to help write this book. People that would know the path and had the commitment to excellence that would transform my goals into this book. I found four great people that deserve more credit that I could possibly acknowledge in this short message of thanks.

The first is with Richard Marek. I found Richard after searching endlessly for a great developmental writer and asked if he would meet with me at a diner in NYC. After three lunches I was able to convince him I was serious and willing to work hard. He accepted by saying, "let's do it." Slowly Richard took on the task on training a fairly poor writer and began chiseling away at the story. Sculpting as we went and constantly forcing me deeper into the story. Patiently and calmly he worked with me to get this story right. Never giving up on his standards of excellence. Along the way we became good friends. He started the task that others could enter to help.

Next was Matthew Ketchum, a professor at Drew University. I had taken a course with Matthew during the pursuit of my Doctorate degree and found him to be both a strong New Testament scholar and an able teacher. Matthew performed both the theological and structural editing of the book. Over the course of a long summer break in 2017, Matthew reviewed each chapter for theological content and provided invaluable insight to the many threads the book contains. While Matthew and I agreed on many aspects of Jesus's mission. Without excess bias, he adjusted to this unique view and his editing stayed committed to the threads of the story, while staying true to the Christian traditions he felt were important.

My copy editor, Richard Willett, was the final piece to the puzzle prior to submission to Post Hill Press. Richard, has edited a number of books, including a *New York Times* bestseller and I was thrilled when he had a window that fit my timing to provide the needed copy editing. Richard fit the bill, no nonsense and very businesslike. His focus on grammatical correctness and the technical aspects of English were critical to finishing the book. Along the way, I found a new friend and a strong professional for my future efforts.

Post Hill Press for accepting the assignment as publisher. From the very start they handled our arrangement with strong business acumen and provided thoughtful insight. Especially Mike Lewis, who while short on words and a minimalist in communication, what he said and how he motivated me to produce the best quality work was inspirational. I have enjoyed working with Post Hill Press, because they understand change, and in fact their business model in the upside down world of publishing provides an author with the best of both traditional and non-traditional publishing. Their commitment to quality and their authors has been a happy marriage.

While the technical and literary assistants have been immeasurable, the commitment from my wife and her extraordinary sense for what was the next step proved to be invaluable advice. At each critical juncture where I would wrestle with what to do next, her simple and commonsense answers unwound many difficult tentacles. Her own personal faith in Jesus has been a lifelong blessing and provided a steady rudder in the creation of this book.

Lastly, thanks to the amazing amount of friends and business associates who provided much of the material through their personal set of ethics and own faith journeys. I am very fortunate to have had so many strong advocates throughout my life.

ABOUT THE AUTHOR

Bruce Hartman is the founder of Gideon Partners, an advisory firm committed to *"Walking with people into a brighter future"* as they navigate life and career transitions and advance Christian values in the marketplace. A seasoned executive with over 30 years of success creating shareholder value for Fortune 500 firms, he graduated in 2013 with a Master of Divinity from Drew University Theological School, earning the Daniel P. Kidder Award for the highest GPA in Pastoral Care.

Offering a rare blend of strategic and tactical business acumen with Christian principles of integrity, camaraderie, and accountability, Hartman fosters professional and business growth while providing actionable insight to strengthen individuals and corporations.

Prior to founding Gideon Partners, he was the Chief Administrative Officer, Executive VP and CFO at Yankee Candle Company, Cushman and Wakefield, and Foot Locker, Inc. where he established global banking and capital market structures and contributed to significant increases in enterprise value. During his tenure at Foot Locker, the company rose from near bankruptcy to solid earnings generation with a stock price increase of 900%.

Hartman's passion for mentoring people throughout his career has enabled him to repeatedly develop talent into C-Suite executives, encourage employee engagement and development at all levels, and transform organizations into high-performing centers of excellence.

He presently serves as President and serves on the Board of Directors of A Future with Hope, as well as, serving on the boards Drew University, and Street Squash, a non-profit providing urban youth with academic enrichment. As President of A Future with Hope, Hartman and the team are helping NJ families rebuild homes impacted by economic and natural disasters. Previously, he was instrumental in significantly growing shareholder value while serving on the Boards of Pathmark Supermarkets and Rue21.

Committed to continuing to explore and share the benefits of the intersection of Christianity, leadership, and career, Bruce is currently pursuing a Doctor of Ministry from Drew University, with a completion date of Spring 2018. Bruce, can be reached at *Brucelhartman.com* and would love to hear your thoughts.